English Grammar for Students of Latin

*The Study Guide
for Those Learning Latin*

Third Edition

Norma W. Goldman

The Olivia and Hill Press®

THE O&H STUDY GUIDES
Jacqueline Morton, editor

English Grammar for Students of Spanish
English Grammar for Students of French
English Grammar for Students of German
English Grammar for Students of Italian
English Grammar for Students of Latin
English Grammar for Students of Russian
English Grammar for Students of Japanese
English Grammar for Students of Arabic
English Grammar for Students of Chinese
Gramática española para estudiantes de inglés

Printed in the U.S.A.

ISBN: 978-0-934034-34-0

Library of Congress Control Number: 2003114557

CONTENTS

CONTENTS

CONTENTS

STUDY TIPS

English Grammar for Students of Latin explains the grammatical terms that are in your Latin textbook and shows you how they relate to English grammar. Once you understand the terms and concepts as they apply to your own language, it will be easier for you to understand what is being introduced in your textbook and by your teacher.

STUDY GUIDE

Before doing an assignment — Read the sections in *English Grammar for Students of Latin* that cover the topics you are going to study in your textbook.

Homework — Take notes as you study your textbook. Highlighting is not sufficient. The more often you write down and use vocabulary and rules, the easier it will be for you to remember them. Complete exercises over several short periods of time rather than in one long session.

Written exercises — As you write Latin words or sentences say them out loud. Each time you write, read, say, and hear a word, it reinforces it in your memory.

In class — Take notes. You will know what the teacher considers important, and it will reinforce what you are studying.

Objective — You have learned something successfully when you are able to take a blank sheet of paper and write a short sentence in Latin using the correct form of the Latin words without reference to a textbook or dictionary. The *Study Tips* below will help you with this learning process.

TIPS FOR LEARNING VOCABULARY

One aspect of language learning is remembering a number of foreign words.

To learn vocabulary — Flashcards are a good, handy tool for learning new words and their meaning. You can carry them with you, group them as you wish, and add information as you advance. Creating your own flashcards is an important first step in learning vocabulary.

1. Write the Latin word or expression on one side of an index card and its English equivalent on the other side.
2. On the Latin side add a short sentence using the word or expression. It will be easier for you to recall a word in

context. To make sure that your sentence is grammatically correct, copy an example from your textbook. For review purposes, note down the chapter and page number of your textbook where the word is introduced.

3. On the Latin side include any irregularities and whatever information is relevant to the word in question.

How to use the cards — Regardless of the side you're working on, always say the Latin word aloud.

1. Look at the Latin side first. Going from Latin to English is easier than from English to Latin because it only requires your recognizing the Latin word. Read the Latin word(s) out loud, giving the English equivalent, then check your answer on the English side.

2. When you go easily from Latin to English, turn the cards to the English side. Going from English to Latin is harder than going from Latin to English because you have to pull the word and its spelling out of your memory. Say the Latin equivalent out loud as you write it down; then check the spelling. Some students prefer closing their eyes and visualizing the Latin word and its spelling.

3. As you progress, put aside the cards you know and concentrate on the ones you still don't know.

How to remember words — Below are suggestions to help you associate a Latin word with an English word with a similar meaning. This first step will put the Latin word in your short-term memory. Use and practice, the next steps, will put the words in your long-term memory.

1. There are many words, called COGNATES, that have the same meaning and approximately the same spelling in English and Latin.

English	Latin
poet	poēta
orator	orātor
temple	templum

2. Try to associate the Latin word with an English word that has a related meaning.

Latin	English	English derivative
māter	mother	maternal
vir	man	virility
patria	fatherland	patriotic

3. If the Latin word has no similarities to English, rely on any association that is meaningful to you. The more associations you have for a word, i.e., the more "hooks," the easier it is for you to remember it. Different types of associations work for different people. Find the one that works best for you. Here are some suggestions:

- Group words by topics or personal associations — It is easier to learn new words if you group them. You can group them according to topics such as food, clothing, activities related to daily life (work, travel, study, the home), or Roman mythology, etc.

- Associate the word with an image — If you have trouble remembering a particular word, you might want to create a "bizarre image" in your mind with which to associate it. This method is very subjective and only works for some people.

> miser = *wretched*
> Scrooge is a **wretched** miser.

> rēgīna = *queen*
> The **queen**, Elizabeth *Regina*, ruled for almost 50 years.

4. To reinforce the Latin word and its spelling, use it in a short sentence.

TIPS FOR LEARNING WORD FORMS

Another aspect of language learning is remembering the various forms a word can take; for example, another form of *book* is *books,* and *do* can take the form of *does.* As a general rule, the first part of the word indicates its meaning and the second part indicates its form.

To learn forms — Paper and pencil are the best tools to learn the various forms of a word. You should write them down until you get them right. The following steps will make learning forms easier.

1. Look for a pattern in the different forms of a word.
- Which letters, if any, remain constant?
- Which letters change?
- Is there a pattern to the changes?
- Is this pattern the same as one you have already learned?
- If this pattern is similar to one you have already learned, what are the similarities and differences?

2. Once you have established the pattern, it will be easy to memorize the forms.
   - Take a blank piece of paper and write down the forms while saying them aloud.
   - Continue until you are able to write all the forms correctly without referring to your textbook.
3. Write short sentences using the various forms.

To review forms — You can use flashcards to review forms as well as to learn them.

Macrons — Some of the vowels in Latin words have a long mark over them called a MACRON. It is an indication that the vowel is to be held longer and pronounced differently from the way in which the unmarked or short vowels are pronounced. It is important to mark and learn the long vowels for the ending of Latin words. Consult your Latin textbook for the pronunciation of short and long vowels.

Norma Goldman

TO THE TEACHER

In our presentation of English grammar, we have avoided projecting Latin grammar onto contemporary English and have followed the current trend in the teaching of grammar in our schools. English nouns, for instance, are no longer identified as having gender. English teachers talk about the function or use of a noun, rather than case. Since these terms and concepts, and many others, are unfamiliar to today's students, we have opted to introduce them as they apply to Latin where, in any event, they are much more developed.

Jacqueline Morton, editor

We wish to pay tribute to Norma Goldman who passed away a few years ago. Norma was a dedicated teacher whose enthusiasm for Latin and Roman culture was appreciated by all. We also wish to thank Krista M. Kulesa, a recent M.A. graduate in Classics at Wayne State University, who reviewed the latest printing of English Grammar for Students of Latin.

WHAT'S IN A WORD?

When you learn a foreign language, in this case Latin,   1
you must look at each word in four ways:
MEANING, PART OF SPEECH, FUNCTION, and **FORM.**

MEANING
An English word may be connected to a Latin word that
has a similar meaning.
> *Mother*, the female head of family, has the same meaning
> as the Latin word **māter.**

Words with equivalent meanings are learned by memorizing   10
VOCABULARY (see pp. 2-3).
Occasionally knowing one Latin word will help you
learn another.
> Knowing that **fīlius** means *son* will help you learn that
> **fīlia** is *daughter.*

Usually, however, there is little similarity between Latin
words, and knowing one will not help you learn another.
As a general rule, you must memorize each vocabulary
item separately.   20
> Knowing that **fēmina** is *woman* will not help you learn
> that **vir** is *man.*

Because so many English words come from Latin, it is
often your knowledge of English that will help you memorize Latin words.

LATIN	MEANING	ENGLISH DERIVATIVE
fīlius	*son*	filial
māter	*mother*	maternal
īnsula	*island*	insular
fāma	*fame*	fame

30

In addition, every language has expressions in which the
meaning of a group of words is different from the meaning of the words taken individually. These are called
IDIOMATIC EXPRESSIONS, or **IDIOMS.** For instance, "*to fall*
asleep" and "*to take* a walk" are English expressions where
"*to fall*" and "*to take*" do not have their usual meaning as
in "*to fall* down the stairs," or "*to take* a book to school."

You will have to be on the alert for these idioms because they cannot be translated word-for-word in Latin.

to fall asleep   dormīre [literally, *"to sleep"*]
to take a walk   ambulāre [literally, *"to walk around"*]

PART OF SPEECH

In English and Latin, words are grouped according to how they are used in a sentence. There are eight groups corresponding to eight PARTS OF SPEECH:

noun	verb
pronoun	adverb
adjective	preposition
conjunction	interjection

Some parts of speech are further broken down according to type. Adjectives, for instance, can be descriptive, interrogative, demonstrative, or possessive. Each part of speech has its own rules for spelling, pronunciation, and use.

In order to choose the correct Latin equivalent of an English word, you will have to identify its part of speech. As an example, look at the word *love* in the following three sentences. In each sentence *love* belongs to a different part of speech, each one corresponding to a different Latin word.

The students *love* to learn the language.
verb = **amant**

My *love* is like a red, red rose.
noun = **amor**

He is famous for writing *love* stories.
adjective = **amātōriās**

The various sections of this handbook show you how to identify parts of speech so that you are able to choose the proper Latin words and the rules which apply to them.

FUNCTION

In English and Latin the role a word plays in a sentence is called its FUNCTION. In order to choose the correct Latin equivalent of an English word, you will have to identify its function. As an example, look at the word *love* in the following sentences. In each sentence *love* has a different function, each one corresponding to a different Latin word.

Our *love* of country is clear.
|
subject = **amor**

He showed his *love* of gold.
|
direct object = **amōrem**

She writes about *love*.
|
object of preposition **dē** (about) = **amōre**

The various sections of this handbook show you how to identify the function of words so that you are able to choose the proper Latin words and the rules which apply to them.

FORM

In English and Latin, a word can influence the form of another word, that is, its spelling and pronunciation. This "matching" is called AGREEMENT and it is said that one word "agrees" with another.

I am   *am* agrees with *I*
she is   *is* agrees with *she*

Agreement does not play a major role in English, but it is an important part of the Latin language. As an example, look at the sentences below where the lines indicate which words must agree with one another.

*The beautiful small **islands** are in the large Mediterranean sea.*

Insulae parvae et pulchrae sunt in magnō marī Mediterrāneō.

In English, the only word that affects another word in the sentence is *islands*, which affects *are*. If the word were *island*, we would have to say *is* to make it agree with *island*.

In Latin, the word for *islands* (**īnsulae**) affects not only the word for *are* (**sunt**), but also the words for *beautiful* (**pulchrae**) and for *small* (**parvae**). The word **in** (*in*) affects the word for *sea* (**marī**) which in turn affects the words for *large* (**magnō**), and for *Mediterranean* (**Mediterrāneō**).

As the various parts of speech are introduced in this handbook, we will go over "agreement" so that you learn which words agree with others and, if they do, how the agreement is shown.

CHAPTER

2

WHAT IS A NOUN?

A **NOUN** is a word that can be the name of
a person, animal, place, thing, event or idea.

- a person   girl, teacher, god, Minerva, Jupiter
- an animal   bull, Cerberus, Minotaur
- a place   island, city, state, Rome, Italy
- a thing   map, sea, picture, star, lamp
- an event   marriage, divorce, birth, death, robbery
  or activity   the Olympics, shopping, rest, growth
- an idea   democracy, humor, hatred, peace
  or concept   time, love, justice, jealousy, poverty

As you can see, a noun is not only a word that names
something that is tangible, i.e., that you can touch, such
as a *map* and a *bull,* but it can also be the name of things
that are abstract, i.e., that you cannot touch, such as
peace, honor and *love.*

A noun that does not state the name of a specific person, place, thing, etc. is called a **COMMON NOUN.** A common noun does not begin with a capital letter, unless it is
the first word of a sentence. All the nouns above that are
not capitalized are common nouns.

A noun that is the name of a specific person, place,
thing, etc. is called a **PROPER NOUN.** A proper noun always
begins with a capital letter. All the nouns in the list above
that are capitalized are proper nouns.

The *king* of *gods* and *men* was *Jupiter.*
     | | | |
common common common proper
 noun   noun   noun   noun

A noun that is made up of two words is called a **COMPOUND
NOUN.** A compound noun can be composed of two common nouns, such as *ice cream.*

IN ENGLISH

To help you learn to recognize nouns, look at the following paragraph where the nouns are in *italics.*

The *Romans,* at the *time* of the *Empire,* imported
goods from *countries* around the *Mediterranean Sea.*

Fancy inlaid *furniture* manufactured in *Asia Minor* decorated the *rooms* of the wealthy *Romans,* while Greek *statues* and finely painted *vases* decorated the *garden* and *atrium. Spices* for *foods* and *medicines* made up a great *market* in *Rome,* and *marble* in various *colors* was imported to decorate the *villas* and *temples.* The unfavorable *balance* of *trade* was so serious under the *Emperor Vespasian* that he set up a special *investigation* to find out why *Rome* was sending out so much *money* for *imports.*

IN LATIN
Nouns are identified and function in the same way as in English.

TERMS USED TO TALK ABOUT NOUNS
- GENDER — In Latin, a noun has a gender; that is, it can be classified according to whether it is masculine, feminine, or neuter (see *What is Meant by Gender?*, p. 10).
- NUMBER — A noun has a number; that is, it can be identified according to whether it is singular or plural (see *What is Meant by Number?*, p. 13).
- FUNCTION — A noun can have a variety of functions in a sentence; that is, it can be the subject of the sentence (see *What is a Subject?*, p. 30) or an object (see *What are Objects?*, p. 36).
- CASE — In Latin, a noun can have a variety of forms depending on its function in the sentence (see *What is Meant by Case?*, p. 22).

✎ **REVIEW**
Circle the nouns in the following sentences.

1. Diana was the goddess of the moon.

2. Phoebus Apollo, her twin brother, was the god of the sun.

3. Mars was the god of war.

4. Juno was goddess of marriage and childbirth.

5. These deities lived on Mt. Olympus, and thus they were called the Olympians.

CHAPTER

3

WHAT IS MEANT BY GENDER?

GENDER in the grammatical sense means that a word can be classified as masculine, feminine, or neuter.

Did Paul give Mary the book?
Yes, *he* gave *it* to *her*.
masc. neuter fem.

Gender is not very important in English; however, it plays a major role in Latin where the gender of a word is often reflected not only in the way the word itself is spelled and pronounced, but also in the way all the words agreeing with it are spelled.

More parts of speech have a gender in Latin than in English.

ENGLISH	LATIN
pronouns	nouns
possessive adjectives	pronouns
	adjectives

Since each part of speech follows its own rules to indicate gender, you will find gender discussed in the chapters dealing with the various types of pronouns and adjectives. In this section we shall only look at the gender of nouns.

IN ENGLISH

While English nouns are not classified according to grammatical gender, the meaning of some nouns reveals the biological sex of the person or animal the noun represents. When we replace a proper or common noun with *he* or *she*, we automatically use *he* for males and *she* for females.

- nouns referring to males indicate the MASCULINE gender

Paul came home; *he* was tired, and I was glad to see *him*.
noun (male)   masculine   masculine

- nouns referring to females indicate the FEMININE gender

Mary came home; *she* was tired, and I was glad to see *her*.
noun (female)   feminine   feminine

All the proper or common nouns that do not indicate a biological gender are considered NEUTER and are replaced by *it*.

The city of Washington is lovely. I enjoyed visiting *it*.
    | |

noun   neuter

IN LATIN

All nouns — common and proper — have a gender; they are either masculine, feminine, or neuter. Latin nouns have not only a natural gender, based on biological sex, but also a grammatical gender, an artificial distinction where no sex is involved.

The gender of common and proper nouns based on **BIOLOGICAL GENDER** is easy to determine. These are nouns whose meaning is tied to one or the other of the biological sexes, male or female.

- all nouns referring to males are masculine

deus	*god*
Iuppiter	*Jupiter*
puer	*boy*

- all nouns referring to females are feminine

māter	*mother*
fīlia	*daughter*
rēgīna	*queen*

The gender of all other nouns, common and proper, is a **GRAMMATICAL GENDER,** unrelated to biological gender, and this gender must be memorized for each noun. Here are some examples of English nouns classified under the gender of their Latin equivalent.

MASCULINE	FEMININE	NEUTER
book	boat	river
chariot	tree	temple
foot	Rome	gift
field	country	animal
mountain	Athens	example

As you learn a new noun, you should always learn its gender because it will affect the spelling and pronunciation of the words related to it. Textbooks and dictionaries usually indicate the gender of a noun with an *m.* for masculine, *f.* for feminine, or *n.* for neuter.

ENDINGS INDICATING GENDER

Gender can sometimes be determined by looking at the ending of the first form of a Latin noun as given in the vocabulary. Below are some endings which often, but not

80 always, correspond to the masculine, feminine, or neuter genders. Since you will see these endings frequently, it is certainly worthwhile to familiarize yourself with them.

MASCULINE ENDINGS

-us	taurus, amīcus, Nīlus	*bull, friend, Nile*
-er	puer, ager, Iuppiter	*boy, field, Jupiter*
-or	auctor, amor, orātor	*author, love, orator*

FEMININE ENDINGS

-a	puella, fēmina, porta	*girl, woman, gate*
-tās	vānitās, aetās, veritās	*vanity, age, truth*
-tūdo	magnitūdo, servitūdo	*great size, slavery*
-iō	regiō, actiō, religiō	*region, action, religion*

90

NEUTER ENDINGS

-um	templum, dōnum	*temple, gift*
-men	flūmen, nōmen	*river, name*
-e	mare	*sea*
-al	animal	*animal*
-ar	exemplar	*example*

 REVIEW

Using the endings listed above, classify the Latin nouns below by circling M (masculine), F (feminine), or N (neuter).

1. alumna *(graduate)*	M	F	N
2. alumnus *(graduate)*	M	F	N
3. exemplum *(example)*	M	F	N
4. orātor *(orator)*	M	F	N
5. Diāna *(Diana)*	M	F	N
6. rosa *(rose)*	M	F	N
7. annus *(year)*	M	F	N
8. flūmen *(river)*	M	F	N
9. porta *(gate)*	M	F	N
10. animus *(soul)*	M	F	N

WHAT IS MEANT BY NUMBER?

NUMBER in the grammatical sense means that a word can be   1
classified as singular or plural. When a word refers
to one person or thing, it is said to be SINGULAR;
when it refers to more than one, it is PLURAL.

> one *book*   two *books*
> | |
> singular   plural

Here are the parts of speech in both languages that have
number.

ENGLISH	LATIN	
nouns	nouns	10
verbs	verbs	
pronouns	pronouns	
demonstrative adjectives	adjectives	

The plural of a word is formed according to different
rules, depending on the part of speech to which it
belongs. In this section we shall only look at the number
of nouns (see *What is a Noun?*, p. 8).

IN ENGLISH

A plural noun is usually spelled and pronounced differently   20
from its singular form. A singular noun is made plural in
one of several ways:

1. a singular noun can add an "-s" or "-es"

> book   book*s*
> kiss   kiss*es*

2. some singular nouns change their spelling

> man   men
> mouse   mice
> leaf   leaves   30
> child   children

Some nouns, called **COLLECTIVE NOUNS**, refer to a group of persons or things, but the noun itself is considered singular.

> A football *team* has eleven players.
> My *family* is well.
> The *crowd* was under control.

IN LATIN

As in English, the singular form of a noun is usually made plural by having its ending changed, although there are words that change internally as well.

- most singular feminine nouns change the ending -a to -ae

SINGULAR	PLURAL		
alumna	alumnae	*graduate*	*graduates (females)*
puella	puellae	*girl*	*girls*

- most singular masculine nouns change the ending -us to -ī

SINGULAR	PLURAL		
amīcus	amīcī	*friend*	*friends*
alumnus	alumnī	*graduate*	*graduates (males)*

- most neuter nouns change the ending -um to -a

SINGULAR	PLURAL		
medium	media	*media*	*media*
datum	data	*data*	*data*

- a few words change the ending -ex or -ix to -icēs

SINGULAR	PLURAL		
index	indicēs	*index*	*indexes/indices*
appendix	appendicēs	*appendix*	*appendixes/appendices*

Consult your textbook for nouns with irregular plurals.

✎ REVIEW

Using the ending changes above, write the plural form of the singular Latin nouns below.

1. alumna　　　　　_____
2. alumnus　　　　_____
3. annus　　　　　_____
4. templum　　　　_____
5. littera　　　　　_____
6. curriculum　　　_____
7. porta　　　　　_____
8. animus　　　　　_____
9. rosa　　　　　　_____
10. codex　　　　　_____

WHAT ARE ARTICLES?

An **ARTICLE** is a word placed before a noun to show whether
the noun refers to a specific person, animal, place, thing,
event, or idea, or whether it refers to an unspecified
person, thing, or idea.

I saw *the* boy you spoke about.
a specific boy

I saw *a* boy in the street.
not a specific boy

IN ENGLISH

In English there are two types of articles, **DEFINITE ARTICLES**
and **INDEFINITE ARTICLES**.

The definite article *the* is placed before a noun which
refers to one or more specific persons, places, animals,
things, or ideas.

I read *the* book you recommended.
a specific book

John likes *the* students in his class.
specific persons

The indefinite article *a* or *an* is placed before a noun
which does not refer to a specific person, place, animal,
thing, or idea (*a* before a noun starting with a consonant,
an before a noun starting with a vowel).

I saw *a* boy in the house.
not a specific boy

I ate *an* apple.
not a specific apple

IN LATIN

There are no articles. When translating a Latin sentence
into English, your knowledge of English and the meaning
of the sentence will help you supply the correct article, or
you may omit the article entirely.

WHAT IS A PRONOUN?

A **PRONOUN** is a word used in place of one or more nouns. It may stand, therefore, for a person, animal, place, thing, event, or idea.

For instance, instead of repeating the proper noun "Midas" in the following sentences, it is more desirable to use a pronoun in the second part of the sentence.

> Midas likes gold, and Midas turns everything to gold.
> Midas likes gold, and *he* turns everything to gold.
> |
>   pronoun

A pronoun can only be used to refer to someone (or something) that has already been mentioned. The word that the pronoun replaces or refers to is called the **ANTECEDENT** of the pronoun. In the example above, the pronoun *he* refers to the proper noun *Midas*. *Midas* is the antecedent of the pronoun *he*.

There are different types of pronouns, each serving a different function and following different rules. Listed below are the more important types and the chapters in which they are discussed.

PERSONAL PRONOUNS — These pronouns replace nouns referring to persons or things that have been previously mentioned. A different set of pronouns is often used depending on the pronoun's function in the sentence.

- subject pronouns (see pp. 30, 41-4)
  > *I* go; *they* read; *he* runs; *she* sings.

- direct object pronouns (see pp. 36-7, 44-6)
  > Midas loves *it*. Pan saw *her*. Apollo killed *them*.

- indirect object pronouns (see pp. 37, 44-6)
  > The goddess gave *him* advice. Send *them* help. Give *her* gifts.

- object of preposition pronouns (pp. 38-9, 44-6)
  > Come with *me*. This gift is for *them*. The Lord be with *you*.

REFLEXIVE PRONOUNS — These pronouns refer back to the subject of the sentence (see pp. 151-2).

> He saw *himself* in the water. They freed *themselves* from danger.

INTERROGATIVE PRONOUNS — These pronouns are used to ask questions (see pp. 143-8).

> *Who* is coming? *What* did the god say? *Whom* did you see?   40

DEMONSTRATIVE PRONOUNS — These pronouns are used to point out persons or things (see pp. 154-5).

> *This (one)* is beautiful. *That (one)* is ugly.
> *These* can be planted now. *Those* are ruined.

POSSESSIVE PRONOUNS — These pronouns are used to show possession or ownership (see pp. 149-50).

> Whose book is that? *Mine. Yours* is on the table.

RELATIVE PRONOUNS — These pronouns are used to introduce relative subordinate clauses (see pp. 156-60).   50

> The god *who* came is powerful.
> The goddess *whom* you worship listens to your prayers.

INDEFINITE PRONOUNS — These pronouns are used to refer to unidentified persons or things.

> *One* should not do that. *Something* is wrong.

Since Latin indefinite pronouns correspond in usage to their English equivalents, there is no special section devoted to them.

IN ENGLISH   60

Each type of pronoun follows a different set of rules.

IN LATIN

As in English, each type of pronoun follows a different set of rules. Latin pronouns are different from English pronouns in that they always reflect case, gender, and number. The rules of agreement are discussed in the sections devoted to the various types of pronouns.

CHAPTER

7

WHAT IS A PREPOSITION?

A **PREPOSITION** is a word that shows the relationship of one word (a noun or pronoun) to another word in the sentence. Prepositions may indicate location, direction, time, manner, or agent.

Paul has an appointment *after* school.
preposition

IN ENGLISH

The noun or pronoun following the preposition is called the **OBJECT OF THE PREPOSITION**. The preposition plus its object form a **PREPOSITIONAL PHRASE**. Prepositions are used to introduce a variety of information:

- to show location

prepositional phrase
Danae was imprisoned *in a dungeon.*
preposition   object of preposition

- to show direction
  Jupiter came *to her* in a shower of gold.
- to show time
  Perseus lived *for many years* on the island.
- to show manner
  Danae reacted **with** *disgust.*
- to show means
  Perseus killed Medusa **with** *a sword.*
- to show agent
  Perseus was given winged sandals **by** *the god Mercury.*

To help you recognize prepositional phrases, here is a story where the prepositional phrases are in *italics* and the preposition which introduces each phrase is in **boldface**.

Because it was foretold that his grandson would kill him, the king **of** *Argos* imprisoned his daughter Danae **in** *a dungeon* so that she would not bear a child. Jupiter, the king **of** *the gods*, fell **in** *love* **with** *her* and came **to** *her* **in** *her prison* **in** *a shower* **of** *gold*. She bore the hero Perseus, but both mother and child were set adrift *in a chest on water.* The chest drifted *to an island* where the two were rescued and taken *to the king.* That king fell *in love with Danae* and wanted to marry her. When grown-up Perseus objected, the king sent him to bring back the head *of Medusa.* Eventually Perseus did kill his grandfather *by accident.*

IN LATIN

Prepositions themselves never change form. However, for each preposition, you must learn if it takes an object in the accusative or ablative case.

> *The chest was carried **toward an island**.*
> Arca **ad īnsulam** portāta est.
> |
>   acc. fem. sing.
>
> **ad** *(toward)* always requires an accusative object

> *The chest was found **by a fisherman**.*
> Arca **ā piscātōre** inventa est.
> |
> abl. masc. sing.
>
> **ā** or **ab** *(by)* requires an ablative object (**ā** before a word beginning with a consonant, **ab** before a word beginning with a vowel)

Some prepositions can take either the accusative or the ablative depending on the way the preposition is used. The preposition **in** *(in, on)*, for instance, is followed by the accusative when motion is indicated by the verb and the ablative when there is no motion.

> *The chest was thrown **into the water**.*
> Arca **in aquam** iacta est.
> |
>   acc. fem. sing.
> motion in the verb *thrown*

> *Danae remained **on the island**.*
> Danaē **in īnsulā** mānsit.
> |
> abl. fem. sing.
> no motion in the verb *remained*

N. B. When learning Latin prepositions, there are several important rules to remember.

1. Do not assume that the same preposition is used in Latin as in English, or even that one is used at all (see pp. 39-40). The Latin case system makes many prepositions which must be used in English unnecessary in Latin (see *What is Meant by Case?*, p. 22).

- *of* (possessive) → genitive (no preposition, see p. 24)

> *The mother **of the boy** is here.*
> Mater **pueī** adest.

- *with* (by means of) → ablative (no preposition, see p. 91)

> *Perseus killed Medusa **with a sword**.*
> Perseus **gladiō** Medūsam necāvit.

- *on, at* (location) → locative (no preposition, see p. 25)

> *They live **at home**.*
> **Domī** habitant.

2. In English, be sure to distinguish between prepositional phrases introduced by *to* indicating the indirect object and *to* indicating direction toward a location.

- *to* indicating an indirect object → dative

The action of the verb is done *to* or *for* someone or something. The prepositional phrase answers the question *to what?* or *to whom?* (see p. 37).

> *He gave a theater **to the city**.*
> *He gave **the city** a theater.*
> > He gave the theater *to what?* To the city.
> > *The city* is the indirect object.
>
> **Urbī** theātrum dōnāvit.
> |
> indirect object → dat. fem. sing.

- *to* indicating direction toward a location → **ad** + accusative

The preposition *to* is used in a phrase of direction towards a location. It answers the question *to where?*

> *He was walking **to the city**.*
> > He was walking *to where?* To the city.
> > *The city* is the object of the preposition *to*. **Ad** *(to)*
> > is followed by the location or destination
> > in the accusative case.
>
> **Ad urbem** ambulābat.
> |
> object of preposition **ad** → acc. fem. sing.

3. In an English sentence or question, remember to restructure dangling prepositions so that you can find the preposition's object and put it in its proper case (see *Dangling prepositions*, pp. 144-5).

> *Who* are you giving the book *to?*
> RESTRUCTURED: *To whom* are you giving the book?
>
> *Who* are you going to play *with?*
> RESTRUCTURED: *With whom* are you going to play?

✎ REVIEW

Underline the prepositional phrases in the sentences below.

■ Indicate what each prepositional phrase would be in Latin: a prepositional phrase (PP), dative indirect object (IO), or a genitive case showing possession (G).

1. Mercury gave winged sandals to Perseus.   PP   IO   G

2. Perseus flew to Gorgon country.   PP   IO   G

3. Perseus cut off the head of Medusa.   PP   IO   G

4. Perseus returned with the Gorgon head.   PP   IO   G

5. Perseus gave the head to the king.   PP   IO   G

6. Perseus freed Danae from the power   PP   IO   G

   of the evil king.   PP   IO   G

WHAT IS MEANT BY CASE?

CASE is the change in the form of a word to show how it functions within a sentence. This change of form usually takes place in the ending of the word; sometimes, however, the entire word changes.

I see John.

John sees *me*.

More parts of speech are affected by case in Latin than in English.

ENGLISH	LATIN
pronouns	nouns
	pronouns
	adjectives

IN ENGLISH

In English the form of a word rarely shows its function in a sentence. Usually it is the word order, where the word is placed in the sentence, which indicates its function and hence shows the meaning of the sentence. We easily recognize the difference in meaning between the following two sentences purely on the basis of word order.

The girl sees the bull on the shore.[1]

Here *the girl* is seeing, and *the bull* is what she sees.

The bull sees the girl on the shore.

Here *the bull* is seeing, and *the girl* is whom it sees.

By placing the nouns *girl* and *bull* in a different part of the sentence we change the meaning of the sentence.

English personal pronouns are a good example of case in English, since their function is indicated not only by their place in a sentence, but also by their form, that is, their case (see *What is a Personal Pronoun?*, p. 41).

I know *them*.

They know *me*.

We do not say, "*I* know *they*" or "*They* know *I*" because the forms "they" and "I" can only be used to refer to the doer of the action (see *What is a Subject?*, p. 30); whereas, "them" and "me" can only be used to refer to the object of the action (see *What are Objects?*, p. 36).

---

[1]Jupiter came to earth as a bull and carried off the maiden Europa to Crete.

In English, there are three cases:

1. The **SUBJECTIVE CASE** is used for personal pronouns which function as subjects or predicate words (see *What is a Predicate Word?*, p. 32).

> *She* came home late.
> |
> personal pronoun
> subject → nominative case

> It is *she*.
> |
> personal pronoun
> predicate word → nominative case

2. The **OBJECTIVE CASE** is used for personal pronouns which function as objects.

> John saw *her* every day.
> |
> personal pronoun
> object → objective case

3. The **POSSESSIVE CASE** is used for nouns and personal pronouns to indicate ownership (see *What is the Possessive?*, p. 34).

> The girl sees the *farmer's* bull on the shore.
> |
> noun possessing the "bull"
> possessive form " 's " added to *farmer*

> I took *mine* and he took *his*.
> | |
> personal pronoun   personal pronoun
> possessive case   possessive case

IN LATIN

Unlike in English, it is not the order in which words appear that reveals the meaning of a sentence. Instead, it is the form of the word itself which reveals its function and, therefore, the meaning of the sentence. Nouns, pronouns, and adjectives change form by taking different endings, called **CASE ENDINGS**, to reflect their function. In this chapter we shall limit ourselves to the case system as it affects nouns.

As long as a noun is put in its proper case, the words in a sentence can be moved around without changing the essential meaning. Look at the three ways the following sentence can be expressed in Latin:

> *The girl sees the bull on the shore.*
> Puella taur**um** in rīpā videt.
> girl   bull   on shore   sees

Taur**um** in rīp**ā** puella videt.
bull   on shore girl   sees

In rīp**ā** taur**um** puella videt.
on shore bull   girl   sees

The endings of the words (boldfaced in the above example) show the case and function of the words in the sentence: "puella" must be the subject and "taurum" must be the object. This makes it evident that *the girl* is doing the looking and *the bull* is what she sees.

Latin nouns, pronouns and adjectives have five main cases (and two minor ones, see Vocative and Locative p. 25), each reflecting a different function of the word in a sentence. Each case also has a singular and a plural form (see *What is Meant by Number?*, p. 13). The list of all these possible forms is called a DECLENSION. When you memorize a declension, the cases are usually in the following sequence:

1. The NOMINATIVE CASE — This is the form in a vocabulary list or dictionary. It is the case used for the subject of a sentence and for predicate words.

> The *girl* looks at the bull.
> |
> subject → **puella** nominative case

> Jupiter is a *god.*
> |
> predicate word → **deus** nominative case

2. The GENITIVE CASE — This form is used to show possession.

> *Cupid's* arrows are sharp.
> |
> possessor → **Cupīdinis** genitive case

3. The DATIVE CASE — This form is used for indirect objects (see p. 37 in *What are Objects?*).

> The girl gave flowers to the *bull.*
> |
> indirect object → **taurō** dative case

4. The ACCUSATIVE CASE — This form is used for most direct objects and for objects of certain prepositions (see p. 39 in *What are Objects?*, and p. 19 in *What is a Preposition?*).

> The bull saw the *girl.*
> |
> direct object → **puellam** accusative case

The girl walked into the *woods.*

object of preposition in *(into)* → **silvam** accusative case

5. The **ABLATIVE CASE** — This form is used for objects of certain prepositions (see p. 39 in *What are Objects?*).

Jupiter is walking with *Mercury.*

object of preposition **cum** *(with)* → **Mercuriō** ablative case

The following two cases are usually omitted from declensions because they generally use forms from other cases.

6. The **VOCATIVE CASE** — This form is used for the person or persons being spoken to.

Europa, beware of the bull!

person being spoken to → **Eurōpa** vocative case

7. The **LOCATIVE CASE** — This form is used for a noun indicating the location of someone or something (see p. 20 in *What is a Preposition?*).

Europa lived *at home* with her father.

location → **domī** locative case

You will have to memorize the case forms for all nouns, pronouns, and adjectives. Fortunately, this is made easy by the Latin system of five declension patterns.

THE DECLENSIONS

Latin nouns are divided into five main groups called the FIRST DECLENSION, the SECOND DECLENSION, the THIRD DECLENSION, the FOURTH DECLENSION, and the FIFTH DECLENSION; hereafter indicated as 1st, 2nd, 3rd, 4th, and 5th. Each declension has its own set of endings to reflect case and number, and some declensions have different sets of endings depending on the noun's gender (see *What is Meant by Gender?*, p. 10). You will have to memorize a sample of the endings for each declension, and that pattern can then be applied to all other words in the same group or declension.

When you learn a new noun, it will usually be introduced in its nominative singular form. You must also memorize its genitive singular form because that form gives you two essentials: the noun's declension and the stem.

1. DECLENSION — The ending of the genitive singular enables you to identify the declension to which the word belongs.

	NOMINATIVE	GENITIVE SINGULAR	GENITIVE SINGULAR ENDING	DECLENSION
	silva *(forest)*	silvae	-ae	1st
	animus *(soul)*	animī	-ī	2nd
	rex *(king)*	rēgis	-is	3rd
	exercitus *(army)*	exercitūs	-ūs	4th
	fidēs *(faith)*	fideī	-eī	5th

2. STEM — The genitive singular minus the ending gives you the stem to which the case endings of each declension are attached.

DECLENSION	GENITIVE SINGULAR ENDING	STEM
1st	silvae	silv-
2nd	animī	anim-
3rd	rēgis	rēg-
4th	exercitūs	exercit-
5th	fideī	fid-

The English derivatives of many Latin nouns are often based on the genitive singular stems and should help you remember the form.

NOMINATIVE SINGULAR	GENITIVE SINGULAR	ENGLISH DERIVATIVE
nōmen *(name)*	nōminis	*nominate*
rex *(king)*	rēgis	*regal*
virgo *(maiden)*	virginis	*virgin, virginal*

Your Latin textbook will give you the endings which are to be added to the stem for each declension. There are a few nouns that are irregular in that they do not follow a specific declension. Your textbook will identify them and you will have to learn them individually.

Since the learning of declensions is important for beginning Latin students, let us go over an example of a noun of the 1st declension to see how the various cases are formed. The principle of the cases will be the same for any word that is declined, whatever the declension.

The vocabulary list in your textbook or the dictionary entry will list a noun as follows:

silva, -ae, *f.*, *forest*

The first form is the nominative singular; the second form, the ending -ae, is that noun's genitive singular ending; the *f.* stands for the gender; and the last word is the English equivalent meaning. These are the steps to follow to establish how that noun is declined.

1. DECLENSION — Identify the declension by the second form listed. The genitive ending "**-ae**" tells you that it is a noun of the 1ˢᵗ declension (see chart p. 26) and that you will have to add the case endings of that declension.
2. GENDER — The "*f.*" tells you that it is a feminine noun. Identifying gender is not difficult for 1ˢᵗ declension nouns which are almost all feminine, except for a few which indicate a male, like **nauta** *(sailor)*. It is important to know the gender of nouns for the declensions where the endings for the same case are different depending on the noun's gender.
3. STEM — Find the stem by taking the genitive singular form and dropping the ending.

   silv-ae
   stem ending

4. ENDING — Add the endings of the first declension listed below.

CASE	SINGULAR	PLURAL
NOMINATIVE	-a	-ae
GENITIVE	-ae	-ārum
DATIVE	-ae	-īs
ACCUSATIVE	-am	-ās
ABLATIVE	-ā	-īs

Thus, the entire declension of the word **silva** reads as follows:

CASE	SINGULAR	PLURAL	USAGE
NOMINATIVE	silva	silvae	*subject or predicate word*
GENITIVE	silvae	silvārum	*possession*
DATIVE	silvae	silvīs	*indirect object*
ACCUSATIVE	silvam	silvās	*direct object or object of preposition*
ABLATIVE	silvā	silvīs	*object of preposition or adverbial expressions*

Notice that the -ā of the ablative singular ending has a long mark called a MACRON over it, indicating that it is a long vowel, i.e. held longer than a short vowel. It is important to mark the long -ā of the ablative singular to differentiate it from the short -a of the nominative singular ending. For pronunciation rules refer to your textbook.

You can apply the above pattern to all the nouns of the 1ˢᵗ declension. Refer to your textbook for the endings of the other declensions. You can follow the same procedure, adding the appropriate endings; the usage of each case is the same.

CHOOSING THE PROPER NOUN FORM

To choose the proper form of a Latin noun in a sentence, you will have to consider the following: its function, its case, its declension, its gender, and its number.

Here are a series of steps you should follow for a sample sentence:

> The girls give the bull flowers.

1. FUNCTION — Determine how each noun functions in the sentence.

girls	→	subject
bull	→	indirect object
flowers	→	direct object

2. CASE — Determine what case corresponds to the function you have identified in step 1.

girls	→	subject	→	nominative case
bull	→	indirect object	→	dative case
flowers	→	direct object	→	accusative case

3. DECLENSION — Identify the declension of each Latin noun based on the ending of the genitive singular.

		GENITIVE SINGULAR		
girls	→	puellae	→	1st declension
bull	→	taurī	→	2nd declension
flowers	→	flōris	→	3rd declension

4. GENDER — Establish the gender of each noun based on the indication in the dictionary or vocabulary list.

girl	→	puella, *f.*	→	feminine
bull	→	taurus, *m.*	→	masculine
flower	→	flōs, *m.*	→	masculine

5. NUMBER — Establish the number of each noun.

girls	→	plural
bull	→	singular
flowers	→	plural

6. SELECTION — Choose the proper form for each noun based on each noun's declension, case, gender, and number.

> Puellae taurō flōrēs dant.

1st	2nd	3rd
nom.	dat.	acc.
fem.	masc.	masc.
pl.	sing.	pl.

N.B. = Nota Bene *(Note well)*
The above is only an introduction to the concept of case. Your Latin textbook will go over all the cases and their various uses in detail.

290

REVIEW

Circle the case that you would use in Latin for the nouns in the sentences below: nominative (N), genitive (G), dative (D), accusative (Acc), or ablative (Abl).

1. The bull carried off Europa to Crete.

bull	→ subject	N	G	D	Acc	Abl
Europa	→ direct object	N	G	D	Acc	Abl
Crete	→ object of preposition **ad** + acc.	N	G	D	Acc	Abl

2. On the island, Europa produced a son.

island	→ object of preposition **in** + abl.	N	G	D	Acc	Abl
Europa	→ subject	N	G	D	Acc	Abl
son	→ direct object	N	G	D	Acc	Abl

3. The name of the son was Minos, and he gave his name to the kings of Crete.

name	→ subject	N	G	D	Acc	Abl
son	→ possessive	N	G	D	Acc	Abl
Minos	→ predicate word	N	G	D	Acc	Abl
name	→ direct object	N	G	D	Acc	Abl
kings	→ indirect object	N	G	D	Acc	Abl
Crete	→ possessive	N	G	D	Acc	Abl

CHAPTER

9

WHAT IS A SUBJECT?

The **SUBJECT** of a sentence is the person or thing
performing the action of the verb.

IN ENGLISH

To find the subject, always look for the verb first; then ask
who? or *what?* before the verb (see *What is a Verb?*,
p. 48). The answer will be the subject of that verb.[1]

> The goddess speaks to the woman.
> VERB: speaks
> *Who* speaks to the woman? ANSWER: The goddess.
> *The goddess* is the singular subject of the verb *speaks*.

> Apollo and Diana are the children of the goddess.
> VERB: are
> *Who* are the children of the goddess? ANSWER: Apollo, Diana.
> *Apollo and Diana* make up the plural subject of the verb *are*.

If a sentence has more than one verb, you have to find
the subject of each verb.

> Latona *calls* her children, and they *kill* the children of Niobe.[2]
> *Latona* is the singular subject of *calls*.
> *They* is the plural subject of *kill*.

Subjects can be located in different places, as you can see
in the following examples (the subject is in **boldface** and
the verb is *italicized*):

> Did **Apollo** *kill* all the sons of the queen?
> Grieving the loss of her children, all alone *stood* **Niobe**.

IN LATIN

As in English, the subject performs the action of the verb.
In Latin, the subject of each verb is put in the nominative
case (see *What is Meant by Case?*, p. 22).

> **Jupiter** *loves* Europa.
> *Who* loves Europa? ANSWER: Jupiter.
> **Iuppiter** Eurōpam amat.
> |
> nom. masc. sing.

---

[1]The subject performs the action in an active sentence, but is acted upon in
a passive sentence (see *What is Meant by Active and Passive Voice?*, p. 89).
[2]Niobe, who had fourteen children, asked the women of the town to pray
to her and not to the goddess Latona who had only two children, Apollo
and Diana. Latona, enraged, sent her children to kill Niobe's children.

The nymphs like the beautiful picture.
> *Who* likes the picture? ANSWER: the nymphs.

Nymphae pictūram pulchram amant.
   |
nom. fem. pl.

Beautiful gifts are pleasing to the goddess.
> *What* is pleasing to the goddess? ANSWER: gifts.

Dōna pulchra sunt deae grāta.   40
 |
nom. neut. pl.

N.B. In English and Latin it is important to find the subject of each verb so that you can choose the form of the verb that goes with that subject. A singular subject takes a singular verb; a plural subject takes a plural verb (see *What is a Verb Conjugation?*, p. 56).

✎ REVIEW

Find the subjects in the sentences below.
- Next to Q, write the question you need to ask to find the subject of the sentences below.
- Next to A, write the answer to the question you just asked.
- Circle if the subject is singular (S) or plural (P).

1. Vesta is the goddess of the sacred fire in Rome.

    Q: _____

    A: _____   S   P

2. The Vestal Virgins tend the sacred fire.

    Q: _____

    A: _____   S   P

3. In the Forum stands the round temple of Vesta.

    Q: _____

    A: _____   S   P

CHAPTER

10

WHAT IS A PREDICATE WORD?

A **PREDICATE WORD** is a word which is connected back to the subject by a **LINKING VERB**, i.e., a verb that is like an equal sign.

Mark is my best friend. [Mark = friend]

subject linking   predicate
        verb   word

IN ENGLISH

The most common linking verbs in English are forms of the verbs *to be, to seem, to appear, to become.* The noun, pronoun, or adjective which follows a linking verb is considered a predicate word (see *What is a Noun?*, p. 8; *What is a Pronoun?*, p. 16; and *What is an Adjective?*, p. 120).

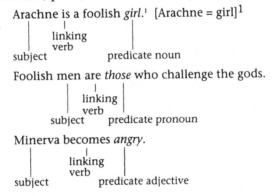

Arachne is a foolish *girl.*[1] [Arachne = girl][1]

linking
verb
subject   predicate noun

Foolish men are *those* who challenge the gods.

linking
verb
subject   predicate pronoun

Minerva becomes *angry.*

linking
verb
subject   predicate adjective

IN LATIN

Most linking verbs are forms of **esse** *(to be)*, **fierī** *(to become)*, and **vidērī** *(to seem)* and the noun, pronoun, or adjective which follows them is a predicate word. It is important that you recognize predicate words since they are in the same case as the subject, namely the nominative.

Arachnē est **puella** stulta.

linking
verb
subject   predicate noun
        ∟ nom. fem. sing. ⌋
*Arachne is a foolish **girl**.*

---

[1]Arachne, a skillful weaver, challenged the goddess Minerva to a weaving contest. The goddess, enraged at the girl's presumption, turned her into a spider.

Hominēs stultī sunt **illī** quī deōs prōvocant.

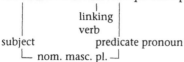

*Foolish men are **those** who challenge the gods.*

40

Minerva fit **īrāta**.

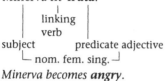

*Minerva becomes **angry**.*

N.B.: In order to choose the proper case in Latin, it is important that you do not confuse predicate words with objects (see *What are Objects?*, p. 36).

50

 REVIEW

Circle the linking verb in the sentences below.
■ Draw an arrow from the predicate word back to the subject.

1. The goddesses are angry.

2. Apollo is a proud god.

3. Daphne is the daughter of a river god.

4. It is he who loves the girl.

5. These are the enemies whom you fear.

CHAPTER

11

WHAT IS THE POSSESSIVE?

The term **POSSESSIVE** means that one noun, the possessor, owns or *possesses* another noun, the possessed.

Mark's Latin book is on the table.
possessor   possessed

IN ENGLISH

There are two constructions to show possession.

1. An apostrophe can be used.

- singular possessor adds an apostrophe + "s"

  Ovid's poetry
  a bird's song
  singular possessor

- plural possessor ending with "s" adds an apostrophe after the "s"

  the boys' mother
  the girls' father
  plural possessor

- plural possessor not ending with "s" adds an apostrophe + "s"

  the children's playground
  the men's department
  plural possessor

2. The word *of* can be used followed by the possessor.

  the poetry *of* Ovid
  singular possessor

  the teacher *of the* students
  plural possessor

IN LATIN

There is only one way to express possession and that is by using the genitive case for the possessor. There is no Latin word for "of" in the sense of possession.

liber **magistrī**

nom.   possessor = genitive singular

the teacher's book (or *the book of the teacher*)

pater **puellārum**   40

nom.   possessor = genitive plural

the girls' father (or *the father of the girls*)

N.B. The word "of" in English does not always imply possession; it can also introduce a description of a noun: "a ship *of this kind*, "a wall *of a hundred feet*." Latin always uses the genitive case for these "of" ideas.

puer **decem annōrum**

      gen. pl.

a boy of ten years   50

Also as an object of the English preposition "of," Latin has a use of the genitive case called **OBJECTIVE GENITIVE**.

Amōrem **pecūniae** dēmōnstrābat.

    gen. sing.

He showed a love of money.

REVIEW

In the sentences below, underline the word or words for which you would use the genitive case in Latin.

- Circle whether the genitive would be the possessive genitive (PG) or the objective genitive (OG).

1. Arachne's skill as a weaver was clear.   PG   OG

2. The foolish girl would not acknowledge
Minerva's superior skill.   PG   OG

3. Arachne showed her love of weaving.   PG   OG

4. Minerva's loom was large and elegant.   PG   OG

5. The nymphs of the forest were the judges.   PG   OG

CHAPTER

12

WHAT ARE OBJECTS?

OBJECTS are nouns or pronouns that receive
the action of the verb. They indicate towards what or whom
the action of the verb is directed.

There are three types of objects: direct objects, indirect objects, and objects of a preposition. In this chapter we have concentrated on noun objects. For additional examples with pronoun objects see pp. 44-6 in *What is a Personal Pronoun?*.

DIRECT OBJECTS
IN ENGLISH

A direct object is a noun or pronoun that receives the action of the verb directly. It answers the question *whom?* or *what?* asked after the verb.

> The god loves *the nymph.*
> The god loves *whom?* The nymph.
> *The nymph* is the direct object.

> The girl sees *the bull.*
> The girl sees *what?* The bull.
> *The bull* is the direct object.

Never assume that a word is the direct object because it comes after the verb. Always ask the question above, and if you do not get an answer, you do not have a direct object in the sentence. Some sentences do not have direct objects.

> The girls work well.
> The girls work whom? No answer possible.
> The girls work what? No answer possible.
> This sentence has no direct object. (*Well* is an adverb telling how the girls worked, see *What is an Adverb?*, p. 141.)

IN LATIN

As in English, a direct object is a noun or pronoun that receives the action of the verb directly. Most English direct objects are put in the accusative case in Latin.

> *The god loves **the nymph**.*
> Deus **nympham** amat.
> |
> direct object → accusative

*The girl sees **the bull**.*
Puella **taurum** videt.
|
direct object → accusative

INDIRECT OBJECTS
IN ENGLISH

An indirect object is a noun or pronoun that receives the action of the verb indirectly, through the prepositions "to" or "for" (see *What is a Preposition?*, p. 18). It explains "to whom" or "for whom," or "to what" or "for what" the action of the verb is done. An indirect object answers the question *to (for) whom?* or *to (for) what?* asked after the verb.[1]

The king gives gifts to *Jupiter* and *Juno*.
The king gives gifts *to whom*? Jupiter and Juno.
Jupiter and *Juno* are two indirect objects.

The farmer did *me* a favor.
The farmer did a favor *for whom*? Me.
Me is the indirect object.

Sometimes the "to" is not expressed in the sentence; it is understood.

John wrote *his brother*.
He wrote *to whom*? His brother.
His brother is the indirect object.

IN LATIN

As in English, an indirect object is a noun or pronoun that receives the action of the verb indirectly. English indirect objects are put in the dative case in Latin.

*The king gives gifts to **Jupiter** and **Juno**.*
Rēx dōna **Jovī** et **Junōnī** dat.
| |
indirect objects → dative

*The farmer did **me** a favor.*
Agricola **mihi** grātum fēcit.
|
indirect object → dative

N.B. Although most Latin verbs take the accusative for the direct object and the dative for the indirect object, some verbs take other cases. Your Latin textbook will indicate these exceptions. Be sure to learn them.

---

[1]Every use of "to" or "for" does not identify an indirect object. These words can also introduce prepositional phrases: *to the island* (**ad īnsulam**), *for wine* (**prō vīnō**), see p. 20.

SENTENCES WITH A DIRECT AND AN INDIRECT OBJECT

A sentence may contain both a direct object and an indirect object, which may be either nouns or pronouns.

IN ENGLISH

When a sentence has both a direct and an indirect object, the following two word orders are possible:

1. subject (S) + verb (V) + indirect object (IO) + direct object (DO)

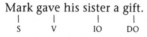

> *Who* gave a gift? Mark.
> *Mark* is the subject.
>
> Mark gave *what?* A gift.
> *A gift* is the direct object.
>
> Mark gave a gift *to whom?* His sister.
> *His sister* is the indirect object.

2. subject + verb + direct object + *to* + indirect object

Marks gave a gift to his sister.
| | | |
S   V   DO   IO

The first structure, under 1, is very common. However, because there is no *"to"* preceding the indirect object, it is more difficult to identify its function than in the second structure.

Regardless of the word order, the function of the words in these two sentences is the same because they answer the same question. Be sure to ask the questions to establish the function of words in a sentence.

IN LATIN

As in English, a sentence can have both a direct and an indirect object. Unlike in English, the word order of the objects is not important since it is the Latin case endings which reveal the function of words. Just make sure that you establish the correct function so that you put the objects in their proper case.

OBJECTS OF A PREPOSITION
IN ENGLISH

An object of a preposition is a noun or pronoun that follows a preposition and is related to it. It answers the question *whom?* or *what?* asked after the preposition.

The tree is *in the forest.*
> The tree is *in what?* The forest.
> *Forest* is the object of the preposition *in.*

This is a story *about Mercury.*
> This is a story *about whom?* Mercury.
> *Mercury* is the object of the preposition *about.*

IN LATIN

As in English, an object of a preposition is a noun or pronoun that follows a preposition and is related to it. In Latin, however, objects of preposition are in the ablative or accusative case depending on the preposition. As you learn new Latin prepositions it is important that you memorize the case each preposition requires.

- **prō** *(before)* + ablative

  *The tree is **before the temple**.*
  > The tree is *before what?* The temple.
  > *Temple* is the object of the preposition *before.*

  Arbor est **prō templō**.
  > |
  > object of preposition **prō** + ablative

- **per** *(through)* + accusative

  *The bear wandered **through the forest**.*
  > The bear wandered *through what?* The forest.
  > *The forest* is the object of the preposition *through.*

  Ursa **per silvam** errābat.
  > |
  > object of preposition **per** + accusative

RELATIONSHIP OF A VERB TO ITS OBJECT

The relationship between a verb and its object is often different in English and Latin. For example, a verb may take an object of a preposition in English but a direct object in Latin. Your textbook, as well as dictionaries, will indicate if a Latin verb needs a preposition before an object.

Here is an example of two English verbs that are followed by a preposition and its object, while the equivalent Latin verbs simply take a direct object in the accusative case. The preposition is part of the meaning of the verb.

- *to look at* → **spectāre** + accusative

  *The girls are looking **at the stars**.*
  > The girls are looking *at what?* The stars.
  > *The stars* is the object of the preposition *at.*

  Puellae **stellās** spectant.
  > |
  > direct object → accusative

130

140

150

160

- *to wait for* → **exspectāre** + accusative

> *The farmers were waiting for **help.***
> The farmers were waiting *for what?* Help.
> *Help* is the object of the preposition *for.*
> Agricolae **auxilium** exspectābant.
> |
>   direct object → accusative

170

N. B. — Avoid translating word-for-word from English to Latin. Remember that Latin has structures different from English. When learning a new Latin verb, check on the case required for its object.

 REVIEW

Underline the objects in the sentences below:
- Next to Q, write the question you need to ask to find the object.
- Next to A, write the answer to the question you just asked.
- Circle the type of object it is: direct object (DO), indirect object (IO), or object of a preposition (OP).

1. The king abandoned his daughter in the woods.

   Q:_____

   A: _____   DO   IO   OP

   Q:_____

   A: _____   DO   IO   OP

2. Wild animals raised Atalanta.

   Q:_____

   A: _____   DO   IO   OP

3. Atalanta, now grown, went to the palace.

   Q:_____

   A: _____   DO   IO   OP

4. The king gave Atalanta his blessing.

   Q:_____

   A: _____   DO   IO   OP

   Q:_____

   A: _____   DO   IO   OP

WHAT IS A PERSONAL PRONOUN?

A **PERSONAL PRONOUN** is a word which replaces a
person or thing that has been mentioned previously.
The word being replaced is called the pronoun's **ANTECEDENT**.

> Here is John. *He* is happy. I envy *him.*
>> *He* is a personal pronoun subject of the verb *is.*
>> *Him* is a personal pronoun object of the verb *envy.*
>> *John* is the antecedent of *he* and *him.*

In English and in Latin, personal pronouns, as well as
other parts of speech, are often referred to by the **PERSON**
to which the pronoun belongs: 1st, 2nd, or 3rd, singular or
plural. The word "person" in this instance is a grammatical
term and each of the six "persons" is used to refer to one
or more persons or things. In the case of the 3rd person
singular, the three pronouns *he, she,* and *it* belong to the
same "person."

Personal pronouns can function as subjects, objects, and
objects of prepositions. In both English and Latin, personal
pronouns have different forms to show the pronoun's
function in the sentence (see *What is Meant by Case?,*
p. 22). We will study the two types of pronouns separately:
pronouns as subjects and pronouns as objects.

PERSONAL PRONOUNS SUBJECTS (see *What is a Subject?*, p. 30)
IN ENGLISH

When a pronoun is used as a subject, the form of the pronoun is said to be in the **SUBJECTIVE** case.

1ST PERSON

I → the person speaking → **SINGULAR**

we → the person speaking plus others → **PLURAL**

> *Mary and I* are free this evening. *We* are going out.

2ND PERSON

you → the person or persons spoken to → **SINGULAR** or **PLURAL**

> *Paul*, do *you* sing folksongs?
> *Peter, Paul and Mary*, do *you* sing folksongs?

3RD PERSON

he, she it → the person or object spoken about → **SINGULAR**

they → the persons or objects spoken about → **PLURAL**

> *Mary and Paul* are free this evening. *They* are going out.

IN LATIN

Latin generally omits the pronouns as subjects, since the personal endings attached to the verb serve the same function (see p. 57 in *What is a Verb Conjugation?*). Only when the subject is stressed, or when the gender of a 3rd person singular subject (**is, ea,** or **id** see below) needs to be indicated, would the Romans have used the pronoun.

When Latin pronouns are used as subjects they are in the NOMINATIVE case. Pronouns are also identified as 1st, 2nd and 3rd persons, each having a singular and plural form. They are usually presented in the following order.

SINGULAR			
1ST PERSON	I	ego	
2ND PERSON	you	tū	
	he	is	(masc.)
3RD PERSON	she	ea	(fem.)
	it	id	(neut.)
PLURAL			
1ST PERSON	we	nōs	
2ND PERSON	you	vōs	
		eī	(masc.)
3RD PERSON	they	eae	(fem.)
		ea	(neut.)

Let us look more closely at the two English subject pronouns *you* and *it,* which have more than one Latin form so that you can learn how to choose the correct one.

"YOU" (2nd PERSON SINGULAR AND PLURAL)

IN ENGLISH

The same pronoun "you" is used to address one or more than one person.

Mary, are *you* coming with me?
Mary and Paul, are *you* coming with me?

IN LATIN

There is a difference between "you" addressing one person (singular) and "you" addressing more than one person (plural).

You are the cause of my grief.

You refers to one person → singular → **tū**
Tū es causa dolōris meī.

You are all my friends.   80
|
You refers to many people → plural → **vōs**
Vōs estis omnēs amīcī meī.

"IT" (3ʳᵈ PERSON SINGULAR)

IN ENGLISH

The pronoun "it" is used to replace a noun referring to
any object or idea.

> My sword is precious. *It* saved my life.
> I love my country. *It* has good citizens.
> Where is that temple? *It* is in the city.   90

IN LATIN

Since Latin nouns have gender, the pronouns which
replace them must also show gender. Thus, a pronoun will
be either masculine, feminine, or neuter depending on
the grammatical gender of the noun which *it* replaces, i.e.,
the gender of its antecedent.

To choose the correct form of *it*, follow these steps.

1. ANTECEDENT — Find the noun *it* replaces.
2. GENDER — Determine the gender of the antecedent in   100
   Latin.
3. FUNCTION — Determine the function of *it* in the sentence.[1]
4. CASE — Choose the case which corresponds to the function found in step 3.
5. SELECTION — Choose the pronoun based on steps 2 and 4.

   My sword is precious. **It** *saved my life.*
   1. ANTECEDENT: sword (**gladius**)
   2. GENDER: **Gladius** is masculine.
   3. FUNCTION: subject of *saved*
   4. CASE: nominative
   5. SELECTION: nominative masculine singular → **is**   110
   Gladius meus est cārus. **Is** vītam meam servāvit.

   I love my country. **It** *has good citizens.*
   1. ANTECEDENT: country (**patriam**)
   2. GENDER: **Patriam** is feminine.
   3. FUNCTION: subject of *has*
   4. CASE: nominative
   5. SELECTION: nominative feminine singular → **ea**
   Patriam amō. **Ea** cīvēs bonōs habet.

---

[1]Since this subsection is about subject pronouns, *it* in all the examples is
a subject. Do not forget that *it* can also be an object (see pp. 44-5).

Where is that temple? **It** *is in the city.*

1. ANTECEDENT: temple (**templum**)
2. GENDER: **Templum** is neuter.
3. FUNCTION: subject of *is*
4. CASE: nominative
5. SELECTION: nominative neuter singular → **id**

Ubi est illud templum? **Id** est in urbe.

PERSONAL PRONOUNS OBJECTS (see *What are Objects?*, p. 36)

IN ENGLISH

When a pronoun is used as a direct object, an indirect object, or an object of a preposition, the form of the pronoun is said to be in the **OBJECTIVE** case.

They invited *him* and *me*.
> They invited *whom*? ANSWER: *Him* and *me*.
> *Him* and *me* are the direct objects of *invited*.

I gave *them* my best work. [I gave my best work *to them*.]
> I gave *to whom*? ANSWER: *To them*.
> *Them* is the indirect object of *gave*.

They are coming *with you* and *her*.
> They are coming *with whom*? ANSWER: *With you* and *with her*.
> *You* and *her* are objects of the preposition *with*.

The form of most pronoun objects is different from the form used as subject. This is one of the few instances in which English shows case. As you can see below, only *you* and *it* have the same form as subjects and objects.

SUBJECTIVE	OBJECTIVE
I	me
you	you
he, she, it	him, her, it
we	us
you	you
they	them

IN LATIN

As in English, Latin has different forms for pronouns used as subjects and objects. However, instead of a single objective case as in English, Latin has four cases of pronouns as objects: the genitive[1], the dative, the accusative, and the ablative. The use of these different cases corresponds to the use of the same cases of nouns (see *What is Meant by Case?*, p. 22).

---

[1]This use of the genitive is an objective genitive (see p. 35).

	SUBJECTS	OBJECTS			
	NOMINATIVE	GENITIVE	DATIVE	ACCUSATIVE	ABLATIVE
PERSON					
			SINGULAR		
1	ego	meī	mihi	mē	mē
2	tū	tuī	tibi	tē	tē
3 MASC.	is	eius	eī	eum	eō
3 FEM.	ea	eius	eī	eam	eā
3 NEUT.	id	eius	eī	id	eō
			PLURAL		
1	nōs	nostrī	nōbīs	nōs	nōbīs
2	vōs	vestrī	vōbīs	vōs	vōbīs
3 MASC.	eī	eōrum	eīs	eōs	eīs
3 FEM.	eae	eārum	eīs	eās	eīs
3 NEUT.	ea	eōrum	eīs	ea	eīs

Remember that the Latin personal pronouns in the 3ʳᵈ person replace nouns having specific genders. Make sure that the gender of the pronoun is the same as the gender of the noun it is replacing (see pp. 43-4).

SUMMARY

To choose the correct form of a personal pronoun to use in a Latin sentence, you have to go through the following steps.

1. PERSON — Determine the person to which the pronoun refers (1ˢᵗ, 2ⁿᵈ, or 3ʳᵈ, singular or plural).
2. GENDER — If the answer to step 1 is the 3ʳᵈ person, determine the gender of the antecedent in Latin.
3. FUNCTION — Determine the function of the pronoun. (If it is an unstressed subject, it can be omitted, see p. 42.)
4. CASE — Determine the case which corresponds to the function found in step 3.
5. SELECTION — Choose the proper form based on steps 1 through 4.

Here are a few examples.

They live in the city.
1. PERSON: 3ʳᵈ person plural
2. GENDER: masculine or feminine
3. FUNCTION: subject (we want to stress men or women)
4. CASE: nominative
5. SELECTION: nominative masculine plural → eī (if *they* refers to men or men and women) or eae (if *they* refers to all women)
Eī (eae) in urbe habitant.

*We see **him**.*
1. PERSON: 3rd person singular
2. GENDER: masculine
3. FUNCTION: direct object
4. CASE: accusative
5. SELECTION: accusative masculine singular → **eum**

Eum vidēmus.

*We gave **her** a letter.*
1. PERSON: 3rd person singular
2. GENDER: feminine
3. FUNCTION: indirect object
4. CASE: dative
5. SELECTION: dative feminine singular → **eī**

Epistulam **eī** dedimus.

*They were writing about **us**.*
1. PERSON: 1st person plural
2. GENDER: masculine and feminine same form
3. FUNCTION: object of preposition *about (**dē**)*
4. CASE: **dē** + ablative
5. SELECTION: preposition **dē** + ablative → **nōbīs**

Dē **nōbīs** scribēbant.

*The Lord be with **you**.*
1. PERSON: 2nd person singular or plural
2. GENDER: masculine and feminine same form
3. FUNCTION: object of preposition *with* (**cum**)
4. CASE: **cum** + ablative
5. SELECTION: preposition **cum** + ablative → **vōbīs** (pl.), **tē** (sing.)

Dominus **vōbīs**cum (**tē**cum).[1]

*The temple is sacred. We worship in **it**.*
1. PERSON: 3rd person singular
2. GENDER: **Templum** *(temple)* is neuter.
3. FUNCTION: object of preposition *in* (**in**)
4. CASE: **in** + ablative
5. SELECTION: preposition **in** + ablative neuter singular → **eō**

Templum est sacrum. In **eō** colimus.

---

[1]Cum is usually attached at the end of the pronoun object to form a single word.

✎ REVIEW

I. Using the chart on p. 45, write the Latin subject and object pronouns you would use to replace the words in *italics*.

1. Children, *you* must all see the temple. _____

2. Mars and Venus, *they* are gods. _____

3. *We* must lay down our arms. _____

4. Venus helped *them* [the women]. _____

5. The gods do not love *her*. _____

II. Determine the Latin equivalent of the word in *italics*.
- Indicate the word's gender in Latin: masculine (M), feminine (N), or neuter (N).
- Indicate the word's number: singular (S) or plural (P).
- Indicate the word's case in Latin: nominative (Nom) or accusative (Acc).

1. The gate is open. Please close *it*.
   Porta *(gate)* is fem.   M   F   N   S   P   Nom   Acc

2. My books are ready. *They* are in my briefcase.
   Librī *(books)* is masc.   M   F   N   S   P   Nom   Acc

3. The gift of the gods is love. Take *it!*
   Dōnum *(gift)* is neut.   M   F   N   S   P   Nom   Acc

CHAPTER

14

WHAT IS A VERB?

1   A VERB is a word that expresses the "action" of the sentence. "Action" is used in the broadest sense, not necessarily physical action.

Let us look at different types of words that are verbs:

- a physical activity   to run, to hit, to talk, to walk
- a mental activity   to hope, to believe, to imagine, to dream, to think
- a state or condition   to be, to feel, to have, to sleep

10   Many verbs, however, do not fall neatly into one of the above three categories. They are verbs, nevertheless, because they represent the "action" of the sentence.

    The book *costs* only $5.00.
    The students *seem* tired.

The verb is the most important word in a sentence. You usually cannot write a COMPLETE SENTENCE, that is, express a complete thought, without a verb.

It is important to identify verbs because the function of the other words in a sentence often depends on their rela-
20   tionship to the verb. For instance, the subject of a sentence is the word doing the action of the verb, and the object is the word receiving the action of the verb (see *What is a Subject?*, p. 30, and *What are Objects?*, p. 36).

IN ENGLISH

To help you learn to recognize verbs, look at the paragraph below where the verbs are in *italics*. Some verbs are single words, and some are verb phrases, that is, a group of words that make up a single verb idea.

    The myth about Jupiter who *came* to earth in the
30   form of a human being *is* familiar to most people. Jupiter, king of the gods, *tested* the hospitality of the people in a certain village. He *had taken* his son Mercury with him, and when the two *had entered* the village and *had sought* refuge for the night in many homes, every home *was closed* to them. The villagers *stoned* the strangers and *set* their dogs on them. Only the old Philemon and his wife Baucis *welcomed* the strangers in their humble cottage. Although they

thought that the strangers *were* poor wanderers, they *set* their best table for them. The gods *thanked* the old couple. Jupiter *transformed* their cottage into a temple and *made* Philemon and Baucis custodians. At their death they *were* both *turned* into trees. The trees still *stand* on either side of the entrance to the temple.

There are two types of verbs depending on whether or not the verb can take a direct object.

- a TRANSITIVE VERB is a verb which takes a direct object. It is indicated in the dictionary by the abbreviation *v.t. (verb transitive).*

    The old couple *welcomed* the strangers.
                v.t.   direct object

- an INTRANSITIVE VERB is a verb that does not take a direct object. It is indicated in the dictionary by the abbreviation *v.i. (verb intransitive).*

    The trees still *stand* on either side of the entrance.
              v.i. (no direct object)

Many verbs can be used both transitively and intransitively, depending on whether or not they have a direct object in the sentence.

    The gods *entered* the house.
        v.t.   direct object

    The gods *entered* and all stood amazed.
         v.i. (no direct object)

IN LATIN

As in English, a verb is a word that shows physical action, a mental activity, or a state or condition.

TERMS TO TALK ABOUT VERBS

- INFINITIVE OR DICTIONARY FORM — The verb form that is the name of the verb is called an infinitive: *to eat, to sleep, to drink* (see *What is the Infinitive?*, p. 53). In the English dictionary a verb is listed without the "to": *eat, sleep, drink.*

- CONJUGATION — A verb is conjugated or changes in form to agree with its subject: *I do, he does* (see *What is a Verb Conjugation?*, p. 56).

- TENSE — A verb indicates tense, that is, the time (present, past, or future) of the action: *I am, I was, I will be* (see *What is Meant by Tense?*, p. 61).

- **MOOD** — A verb shows mood, that is the speaker's attitude toward what he or she is saying (see *What is Meant by Mood?*, p. 93).
- **VOICE** — A verb shows voice, that is, the relation between the subject and the action of the verb (see *What is Meant by Active and Passive Voice?*, p. 89).
- **PARTICIPLE** — A verb may be used to form a participle: *writing, written; singing, sung* (see *What is a Participle?*, p. 78).
- **TRANSITIVE** OR **INTRANSITIVE** — A verb can be classified as transitive or intransitive depending on whether or not the verb can take a direct object (see p. 49).

90

✎ REVIEW

Underline the verbs or verb phrases in the following sentences.
- Circle whether the verb is transitive (V.T.) or intransitive (V.I.)

1. Niobe praises her children.	V.T.	V.I.
2. Juno is watching her husband.	V.T.	V.I.
3. Daphne was running fast.	V.T.	V.I.
4. Jupiter loved many females.	V.T.	V.I.
5. Diana kills all of Niobe's children.	V.T.	V.I.

15

WHAT ARE THE PRINCIPAL PARTS
OF A VERB?

The PRINCIPAL PARTS of a verb are the forms we need   1
in order to create all the different tenses.

IN ENGLISH
English verbs have three principal parts:
1. the infinitive without "to"
2. the past tense
3. the past participle

If you know these parts, you can form all the other tenses
of that verb (see *What is an Infinitive?*, p. 53; *What is the
Past Tense?*, p. 65, and p. 81 in *What is a Participle?*).   10
English verbs fall into two categories depending on how
they form their principal parts:

1. REGULAR VERBS—These verbs are called regular because
their past tense and past participle forms follow the predictable pattern of adding -*ed*, -*d*, or -*t* to the infinitive.

INFINITIVE	PAST TENSE	PAST PARTICIPLE
to walk	walk*ed*	walk*ed*
to seem	seem*ed*	seem*ed*
to burn	burn*ed* (burn*t*)	burn*ed* (burn*t*)

Since the past tense and the past participle are identical,   20
regular verbs have only two principal parts, the infinitive and the past.

2. IRREGULAR VERBS—These verbs are called irregular because
their principal parts do not follow a regular pattern.

INFINITIVE	PAST TENSE	PAST PARTICIPLE
to be	was	been
to sing	sang	sung
to go	went	gone
to write	wrote	written

IN LATIN   30
Latin verbs have four principal parts:
1. the 1st person singular of the present tense
2. the infinitive
3. the 1st person singular of the perfect tense
4. the perfect passive participle

40

In the vocabulary of your textbook and in the dictionary a verb entry for the verb *to love* would look as follows: **amō, -āre, -āvī, -ātum**, with part of the stem or base (**am-**) understood to be continued for each form (**amāre, amāvī, amātus, -a, -um**).

The first principal part (**amō**) is the 1st person singular of the present tense *(I love, am loving, do love)*. It is the form under which a verb is listed in a vocabulary or dictionary.

The second principal part (**amāre**) is the infinitive *(to love)*, which indicates the conjugation to which the verb belongs, and which, with the **-re** dropped (**amā-**), provides the present stem of the verb on which the present, imperfect, and future tenses are based.

50

The third principal part (**amāvī**) is the 1st person singular of the perfect tense *(I loved, have loved, did love)*. It provides the stem (**amāv-**) for the perfect system (all the perfect tenses: perfect, past perfect, and future perfect).

The fourth principal part (**amātus, -a, -um**) is the perfect passive participle *(having been loved)*, used as a verbal adjective (see p. 82) and to make the perfect tenses in the passive voice (see *Perfect tenses in the passive voice*, p. 91).

You will find additional information on the principal parts in the chapters dealing with the various verb tenses.

 REVIEW

I. Write the principal parts of these English verbs.

INFINITIVE	PAST TENSE	PAST PARTICIPLE
1. to think	_____	_____
2. to run	_____	_____
3. to drive	_____	_____

II. Using the principal parts of the regular verb *love*, **amō, amāre, amāvī, amātus (-a, -um)**, as an example, write the principal parts of the regular verb **laudō** *(praise)*.
   ▪ Write the English translations of the principal parts above.

	PRESENT TENSE 1ST PER. SING.	INFINITIVE	PERFECT TENSE 1ST PER. SING.	PERFECT PASSIVE PARTICIPLE
LATIN	_____	_____	_____	_____
ENGLISH	_____	_____	_____	_____
	_____		_____	
	_____		_____	

WHAT IS THE INFINITIVE?

The INFINITIVE is a form of the verb without person or number, giving its basic meaning. ¹

The Latin equivalent of the verb *to study* is **discere**.
    infinitive

IN ENGLISH

All verbs have two infinitives: a present infinitive and a perfect infinitive.

PRESENT INFINITIVE — The present infinitive is composed of two words: *to* + the dictionary form of the verb: *to love, to walk*. The DICTIONARY FORM is the form of the verb that is listed as the entry in the dictionary: *love, walk*. ¹⁰

PERFECT INFINITIVE — The perfect inifnitive is composed of *to have* + the past participle (see p. 81 in *What is a Participle?*): *to have loved, to have walked*.

PRESENT INFINITIVE	PERFECT INFINITIVE
to be	to have been
to write	to have written
to love	to have loved

Although the infinitive is the most basic form of the verb, it can never be used in a sentence without another verb that is conjugated (see *What is a Verb Conjugation?*, p. 56). ²⁰

To learn is challenging.
infinitive conjugated verb

It *is* important *to be* on time.
conjugated verb infinitive

Mark and Julia *want to come* home.
    conjugated verb infinitive ³⁰

The dictionary form of the verb, rather than the infinitive, is used after such verbs as *let, must, should,* and *can*.

Mark *must come* home by midnight.
    dictionary form

Apollo *let* his son *drive* the chariot of the sun.
    dictionary form

IN LATIN

As in English, all verbs have a present infinitive and a perfect infinitive. Latin also has a future infinitive.

PRESENT INFINITIVE — The present infinitive, the second principal part of the verb, ends in **-re** (see *What are the Principal Parts of a Verb?*, p. 51). The present infinitive form provides two essential elements.

    1. CONJUGATION — The ending of the present infinitive enables you to identify the conjugation to which the verb belongs: 1st **-āre**, 2nd **-ēre**, 3rd **-ere**, or 4th **-īre**.

    2. PRESENT STEM — The stem of the present infinitive, referred to as the **PRESENT STEM**, gives you the stem to which are attached the personal endings of the present tense, as well as the tense signs and personal endings for the imperfect and future tenses. (See *What is the Present Tense?*, p. 63, *What is the Past Tense?*, p. 65, and *What is the Future Tense?*, p. 71.)

PERFECT INFINITIVE — The perfect infinitive is formed by adding **-isse** to the perfect stem of the verb (see pp. 66).

	PRESENT INFINITIVE	PERFECT INFINITIVE	
1st	amāre	amāvisse	*to love, to have loved*
2nd	docēre	docuisse	*to teach, to have taught*
3rd	capere	cēpisse	*to take, to have taken*
4th	venīre	vēnisse	*to come, to have come*

FUTURE INFINITIVE — The future infinitive is a verb phrase formed by adding the ending **-ūrus, -a, -um** to the present stem + **esse**. It is mainly used in indirect statements (see p. 111 in *What is Meant by Direct and Indirect Statements?*).

    amātūrus esse   *about to love*

The present infinitive has three main functions:

- as a complementary infinitive; i.e., to complete the meaning of a conjugated verb

    *Mark and Julia want **to come** home.*
    Marcus et Iūlia domum **venīre** dēsīderant.
                 infinitive conjugated verb

- as a noun, particularly as subject of a sentence (see *What is a Subject?*, p. 30)

    To learn *is easy.*
    Discere est facile.
        infinitive conjugated verb

■ as a verb in an indirect statement (see p. 111)

80

> *He says that the gods are coming.*
> Dīcit deōs **venīre.**
> verb of saying   infinitive

CONSULTING THE DICTIONARY

In English it is possible to change the meaning of a verb by placing short words (prepositions or adverbs) after it. For example, the verb *look* in Column A below changes meaning depending on the word that follows it *(to, after, for, into)*. In Latin it is impossible to change the meaning of a verb by adding a preposition or an adverb as in Column A. An entirely different Latin verb corresponds to each meaning.

90

COLUMN A		MEANING	LATIN
to look	→	to look at I *looked at* the photo.	**spectāre**
to look for	→	to search for I *am looking for* my book.	**quaerere**
to look after	→	to take care of I *am looking after* the children.	**cūrāre**
to look into	→	to investigate We'*ll look into* the problem.	**investigāre**

100

When consulting an English-Latin dictionary, all the examples above under Column A can be found under the dictionary entry *look* (**spectāre**); however, you will have to search under that entry for the specific expression to find the correct Latin equivalent.

 REVIEW

Give the English infinitive for the italicized verbs below.

1. Apollo *gave* Midas ass's ears. _____

2. His barber *knew* the secret. _____

3. His barber *was* the only one who *saw* the ears. _____

_____

4. He *dug* a hole in the ground. _____

5. He *whispered* the secret into the hole. _____

6. The reeds in the hole *sang* the secret aloud. _____

CHAPTER

17

WHAT IS A VERB CONJUGATION?

A VERB CONJUGATION is a list of the six possible forms
of the verb for a particular tense.

> I am
> you are
> he, she, it is
> we are
> you are
> they are

Different tenses have different verb forms, but the principle
of conjugation remains the same. In this chapter all our
examples are in the present tense (see *What is the Present
Tense?*, p. 63).[1]

IN ENGLISH

The verb *to be* conjugated above is the English verb that
changes the most; it has three forms: *am, are,* and *is*. (The
initial vowel is often replaced by an apostrophe: *I'm,
you're, he's*). Most English verbs only have two forms such
as the verb *to love*.

SINGULAR	
1ST PERSON	I *love*
2ND PERSON	you *love*
3RD PERSON	he *loves* she *loves* it *loves*
PLURAL	
1ST PERSON	we *love*
2ND PERSON	you *love*
3RD PERSON	they *love*

Because English verbs change so little, it isn't necessary to
learn "to conjugate a verb;" that is, to list all its possible
forms. For most verbs, it is much simpler to say that the
verb adds an "-s" in the 3rd person singular.

IN LATIN

The word *conjugation* comes from two Latin ideas: **con** *(with)*
and **jug** *(join)*; the endings are joined to the stem of the verb

---

[1]Unless otherwise specified, all tenses are in the active voice (see *What is
Meant by Active and Passive Voice?*, p. 89).

resulting in a verb form. Unlike English verb forms, Latin verb forms change endings to indicate the different persons (1ˢᵗ, 2ⁿᵈ, and 3ʳᵈ) and number (singular and plural). (See *What is a Personal Pronoun?*, p. 41).

The first step is to establish whether the verb is a regular or irregular verb.

- Almost all verbs follow a predictable pattern and are called REGULAR VERBS. Only one example must be memorized, and the pattern can then be applied to other verbs in the same group.

- A few verbs do not follow a predictable pattern and are called IRREGULAR VERBS. The conjugation of these verbs must be memorized individually. Some common verbs are irregular, for instance **esse** *(to be)*. Consult your textbook for the conjugation of irregular verbs.

For each tense, a Latin verb has six different endings, one for each person in the singular and in the plural. These endings are called PERSONAL ENDINGS. Let us look at the conjugation of the regular verb **amāre** *(to love)* in the present tense.

SINGULAR

1ˢᵗ PERSON	amō	*I love, I am loving, I do love*
2ⁿᵈ PERSON	amās	*you love, you are loving, you do love*
3ʳᵈ PERSON	amat	*he, she, it loves; he, she, it is loving; he, she, it does love*

PLURAL

1ˢᵗ PERSON	amāmus	*we love, we are loving, we do love*
2ⁿᵈ PERSON	amātis	*you love, you are loving, you do love*
3ʳᵈ PERSON	amant	*they love, they are loving, they do love*

Since the personal endings of the verb indicate the subject, Latin subject pronouns do not usually have to be expressed: the 1ˢᵗ person singular **amō** can only mean "*I* love." In the 3ʳᵈ person singular, however, the -t personal ending may refer to a masculine, feminine, or neuter subject: **amat** can mean "*he* loves, *she* loves," or "*it* loves." In this case, you will have to look at the previous sentences, i.e., the CONTEXT, to identify the subject.

Marcus flōrēs portat. Flōrēs **amat.**
Mark is carrying the flowers. He loves the flowers.

Iūlia flōrēs portat. Flōrēs **amat.**
Julia is carrying the flowers. She loves flowers.

Animal flōrēs dēvorat. Flōrēs **amat.**
The animal is eating the flowers. It loves flowers.

HOW TO CONJUGATE A REGULAR VERB

80 Regular verbs are conjugated according to one of four patterns, or groups (also called "conjugations"), referred to as the **1ˢᵀ CONJUGATION**, the **2ᴺᴰ CONJUGATION**, the **3ᴿᴰ CONJUGATION**, and the **4ᵀᴴ CONJUGATION**. To conjugate a regular verb these are the steps to follow.

1. CONJUGATION — Establish the conjugation of the verb by looking at the vowel that precedes the **-re** of the infinitive (see *What is the Infinitive?*, p. 53).

CONJUGATION	INFINITIVE ENDING		
90	1ˢᵗ	-āre	amāre	*to love*
2ⁿᵈ	-ēre	docēre	*to teach*
3ʳᵈ	-ere	mittere	*to send*
4ᵗʰ	-īre	audīre	*to hear*

It is important to distinguish between the long and short **-e-** in the infinitive of verbs, because they indicate the difference between the 2ⁿᵈ and 3ʳᵈ conjugations. Your Latin textbook will also refer to a category of 3ʳᵈ conjugation verbs called **3ʳᵈ-iō**, so called because a characteristic **-i-** appears in several forms: **faciō** *(I do, I make)*, **faciēbam** *(I did, I made)*, **faciam** *(I shall make)*. The 3ʳᵈ-iō verbs take the usual 3ʳᵈ conjugation personal endings.

100

2. STEM — Determine the present stem to which you will add the personal endings by dropping the **-re** ending of the infinitive (see p. 54).

CONJUGATION	INFINITIVE	STEM
1ˢᵗ	amāre	amā-
2ⁿᵈ	docēre	docē-
3ʳᵈ	mittere	mitte-
4ᵗʰ	audīre	audī-

110 The present stem is used for the present tense (see p. 63). the imperfect tense (pp. 65-6), and the future tense (p. 71). Consult your textbook for irregularities and for the stems to be used for other tenses.

3. PERSONAL ENDINGS — Add the personal endings you have memorized.

PERSON	SINGULAR	PLURAL
1ˢᵗ	-ō or -m[1]	-mus
2ⁿᵈ	-s	-tis
3ʳᵈ	-t	-nt

[1]-**m** appears in the imperfect and future tenses.

These personal endings are the same for the present, imperfect, and future tenses of all four conjugations. In order to distinguish between these tenses which have the same stem and personal endings, one or two letters, called a TENSE SIGN, are inserted between the stem and the personal endings in the imperfect (see p. 65) and in the future tenses (see p. 71). Consult your textbook for irregularities and for the endings to be used for other tenses. [120]

Let us look at other regular verbs belonging to the same conjugation to see how a pattern is applied. [130]

amāre	to love
portāre	to carry
cantāre	to sing

1. CONJUGATION — The -ā- which precedes the -re infinitive ending indicates that they belong to the 1ˢᵗ conjugation.

2. STEM — Dropping the -re ending of the infinitive gives us the present stem of each verb.
    amā-
    portā-
    cantā- [140]

3. PERSONAL ENDINGS — The same personal endings are added to the stem of each verb to form the present tense.

PERSON
SINGULAR

1ˢᵗ	amō [1]	portō [1]	cantō [1]
2ⁿᵈ	amās	portās	cantās
3ʳᵈ	amat	portat	cantat

PLURAL

1ˢᵗ	amāmus	portāmus	cantāmus
2ⁿᵈ	amātis	portātis	cantātis
3ʳᵈ	amant	portant	cantant

[150]

Your Latin textbook lists the complete pattern for the other three conjugations.

---

[1]The 1ˢᵗ person singular in the 1ˢᵗ conjugation contracts the final -a of the stem + the personal ending ō to ō→ **amō.**

REVIEW

I. Circle the infinitive ending for each Latin verb below.
- Circle the conjugation to which each verb belongs.

1. cantāre *(to sing)*	1st	2nd	3rd	4th
2. vīvere *(to live)*	1st	2nd	3rd	4th
3. dēbēre *(to owe)*	1st	2nd	3rd	4th
4. mūnīre *(to fortify)*	1st	2nd	3rd	4th
5. crēdere *(to believe)*	1st	2nd	3rd	4th

II. The Latin equivalent of the verb *to praise* is **laudāre**.
- Indicate the stem.
- Write the Latin present tense conjugation of the verb.
- Write a simple English translation for each form.

STEM: _____

1ST PER. SING.   _____ _____

2ND PER. SING.   _____ _____

3RD PER. SING.   _____ _____

1ST PER. PL.   _____ _____

2ND PER. PL.   _____ _____

3RD PER. PL.   _____ _____

WHAT IS MEANT BY TENSE?

The TENSE of a verb indicates when the action of the verb takes place: at the present time, in the past, or in the future. The word *tense* comes from the Latin **tempus**, meaning *time.*

you eat	PRESENT
you ate	PAST
you will eat	FUTURE

As you can see, just by putting the verb in a different tense and without giving any additional information (such as "you eat *now*," "you ate *yesterday*," "you will eat *tomorrow*"), one can indicate when the action of the verb takes place.

Tenses may be classified according to the way they are formed. A SIMPLE TENSE consists of only one verb form: *ate,* while a VERB PHRASE consists of one or more auxiliaries plus the main verb: *am eating* (see *What are Auxiliary Verbs?*, p. 75).

IN ENGLISH

Listed below are the main six tenses in English.

PRESENT	I eat	PRESENT PERFECT	I have eaten
PAST	I ate	PAST PERFECT	I had eaten
FUTURE	I will eat	FUTURE PERFECT	I will have eaten

As you can see, there are only two simple tenses (present and past). The other tenses are verb phrases. The listing of the forms of a verb in all six tenses is called a SYNOPSIS. Above is a synopsis of the verb *eat* in the 1ˢᵗ person singular.

IN LATIN

In Latin, the same six tenses are divided into two systems, depending on whether the present stem (see p. 54) or perfect stem (see p. 66) is used to form the tense.

PRESENT SYSTEM	PERFECT SYSTEM
present	perfect
imperfect	past perfect or pluperfect
future	future perfect

These tenses are discussed in separate sections: *What is the Present Tense?*, p. 63; *What is the Past Tense?*; p. 65; *What is the Past Perfect Tense?*; p. 69, *What is the Future Tense?*, p. 71; and *What is the Future Perfect Tense?*, p. 73.

REVIEW

I. Write a synopsis in the 1ˢᵗ person singular ("I") for the English verb *think*.

PRESENT_____   PRESENT PERFECT_____

PAST   _____   PAST PERFECT _____

FUTURE _____   FUTURE PERFECT _____

II. Write a synopsis in the 3ʳᵈ person plural ("they") for the English verb *eat*.

PRESENT_____   PRESENT PERFECT_____

PAST   _____   PAST PERFECT _____

FUTURE _____   FUTURE PERFECT _____

WHAT IS THE PRESENT TENSE?

The **PRESENT TENSE** indicates that the action is happening
at the present time. It can be at the moment the speaker
is speaking, a habitual action, or a general truth.

PRESENT TIME	I *see* you.
HABITUAL ACTION	He *smokes* constantly.
GENERAL TRUTH	The sun *rises* every day.

IN ENGLISH

There are three forms of the verb that indicate the present
tense. Each form has a slightly different meaning:

SIMPLE PRESENT	Pan *watches* the nymph.
PRESENT PROGRESSIVE	Pan *is watching* the nymph.
PRESENT EMPHATIC	Pan *does watch* the nymph.

To ask questions, you need to use the progressive or
emphatic form.

Is Pan *watching* the nymph?
Does Pan usually *watch* the nymph?

IN LATIN

Unlike in English, there is only one verb form to indicate
the present tense. The Latin present tense is used to
express the meaning of the simple, progressive, and
emphatic forms of the English present tense.

The present tense in Latin is a simple tense formed by
adding a set of personal endings to the present stem of the
verb (see p. 58 and *What is a Verb Conjugation?*, p. 56).

*Pan **watches** the nymph.*
    |
    spectat

*Pan **is watching** the nymph.*
    └──┬──┘
    spectat

*Pan **does watch** the nymph.*
    └──┬──┘
    spectat

When translating a Latin verb in the present tense into
English, you will have to choose the most appropriate of
the three English meanings according to the context.

N. B. Since the Latin present is always indicated by the stem plus the ending of the verb without an auxiliary verb such as *is* and *does,* do not translate these English auxiliary verbs into Latin. Simply put the main verb in the present tense.

40

 REVIEW

Below are three Latin sentences followed by their English translation.
- Write the English translation for each verb in the progressive form.
- Write the English translation for each verb in the emphatic form.
- Write each sentence in English as a question.

1. Puellae aquam sacram **portant**.
   *The girls **carry** the sacred water.*

   PROGRESSIVE FORM: _____

   EMPHATIC FORM: _____

   QUESTION: _____?

2. Virgō Vestālis ignem sacram **cūrat**.
   *The Vestal Virgin **takes care** of the sacred fire.*

   PROGRESSIVE FORM: _____

   EMPHATIC FORM: _____

   QUESTION: _____?

3. Virginēs Vestālēs in aede sacrā **habitant**.
   *The Vestal Virgins **live** in a sacred building.*

   PROGRESSIVE FORM: _____

   EMPHATIC FORM: _____

   QUESTION: _____?

WHAT IS THE PAST TENSE?

The **PAST TENSE** is used to express an action [1]
that occurred previously, some time before the present time.

I *saw* you yesterday.

IN ENGLISH

There are several verb forms which indicate that the
action took place in the past.

SIMPLE PAST	I worked
PAST PROGRESSIVE	I was working
PAST EMPHATIC	I did work
WITH HELPING VERB USED TO	I used to work [10]
PRESENT PERFECT	I have worked

The simple past is a **SIMPLE TENSE**; that is, it consists of one
word (*worked* in the example above). The other past tenses
are called **VERB PHRASES**; i.e., they consist of more than one
word, an auxiliary verb plus a main verb: *was working, did
work, have worked* (see *What is an Auxiliary Verb?*, p. 75).

IN LATIN

There are two Latin tenses which correspond to the several
verb forms above: the imperfect and the perfect (present [20]
perfect in English).

THE IMPERFECT TENSE

The imperfect is a simple tense formed with the present
stem + the imperfect tense sign -**bā**- + personal endings
(see pp. 57-9). The personal endings are the same as those
of the present tense, except that the 1st person singular
ends in -**m** (spectā- + -ba- + m → spectābam *(I watched)*.

There are several English verb forms that indicate that
the imperfect should be used in Latin.

1. when the English verb form is in the past progressive [30]
tense *(were watching)*

*The nymphs **were watching** the stag in the woods.*
Nymphae cervum in silvīs **spectābant**.
                                    |
                              imperfect

2. when the English verb form is in the past emphatic tense
   (did work)

> *The women **did work** in the fields for a long time.*
> Diū fēminae in agrīs **labōrābant**.
> |
>   imperfect

3. when the English verb form includes, or could include,
   the helping verb "used to" or "was accustomed to" *(used
   to work, was accustomed to work)*

> *Narcissus **used to watch** his reflection in the pool.*
> Narcissus in stagnō imāginem suam **spectābat**.
> |
>   imperfect

THE PERFECT TENSE

The perfect tense of all four conjugations is formed with a
PERFECT STEM based on the third principal part of the verb
and a special set of perfect personal endings.

1. PRINCIPAL PART — Identify the third principal part of a
   verb (see *What are the Principal Parts of a Verb?*, p. 51).

> amō, amāre, amāvī, amātum
> |
>   3ʳᵈ principal part → perfect

2. PERFECT STEM — To find the perfect stem, drop the final
   -ī of the third principal part.

> amāv-

The perfect stem is not only the stem to which the perfect personal endings (see 3 below) are added to form
the perfect tense; it also serves as the stem to form the
past perfect and future perfect tenses (see (*What is the
Past Perfect Tense?*, p. 69 and *What is the Future Perfect
Tense?*, p. 73).

3. PERSONAL ENDINGS — Add the perfect personal endings.
   They are the same for all the conjugations.

PERSON	SINGULAR	PLURAL
1ˢᵗ	-ī	-imus
2ⁿᵈ	-istī	-istis
3ʳᵈ	-it	-ērunt

The perfect tense has several English translations; for
example **amāvī** can be translated *I loved, I have loved,* and
I did love.

SELECTION OF THE IMPERFECT OR PERFECT TENSE

When discussing and describing past events and activities, both the imperfect and the perfect are used. Whether to put a verb in the perfect or the imperfect tense often depends upon the context. As a general guideline, the difference in the two tenses is as follows:

IMPERFECT → tells "how things used to be" or "what was going on" during a period of time

PERFECT → tells "what happened" during a fixed period of time

Here is an example. In English, the same form of the verb *to go,* namely "went," is used in the two answers below: "I *went* to the park." However, the tense of the Latin verb **īre** *(to go)* changes depending on the question asked.

- "What happened?"

    QUESTION: *What **did** you do yesterday?*
    ANSWER: *I **went** to school.*
    > The question and answer tell "what happened yesterday;" therefore, the Latin equivalent of *did do* and *went* are in the perfect.

    QUESTION: Quid **ēgistī** heri?
    ANSWER: **Īvī** in scholam.

- "How things used to be"

    QUESTION: *What **did** you all do when you were children?*
    ANSWER: *We **went** to school.*
    > The question and answer tell "how things used to be;" therefore, the Latin equivalent of *did do* and *went* are in the imperfect.

    QUESTION: Quid **agēbātis** quandō līberī erātis?
    ANSWER: **Ībāmus** in scholam.

- "What was going on?"

    Since the perfect and the imperfect indicate actions that took place at some time in the past, often during the same period, you will often find the two tenses intermingled in a sentence or a story.

    *Callisto **was walking** in the woods when she **saw** a bear.*
    > Both actions *was walking* and *saw* took place at the same time in the past. What was going on? *Callisto **was walking*** → imperfect. What happened? *She **saw** a bear* → perfect.

    Callistō per silvās **ambulābat** cum ursam **vīdit.**
    imperfect   perfect

80
90
100
110

120
Consult your Latin textbook for additional guidelines to help you choose the appropriate tense. Practice by analyzing English paragraphs. Pick out the verbs in the past and indicate for each one if you would put it in the perfect or the imperfect. Sometimes both tenses are possible, but usually one of the two is more logical.

 REVIEW

Circle the verbs in *italics* that would be put in the Imperfect and underline the verbs in *italics* that would be put in the Perfect in Latin.

I *was sitting* at home in the evening watching television. The dog *was sleeping* beside me, and I *was* not afraid because he *was* a good watch dog. My husband *was working* late, and my son *was sleeping* upstairs. Suddenly I *heard* a noise in the kitchen. The dog *sat up* and *barked*. *I* *ran* upstairs and *called* the police on the phone. They *arrived* in minutes and *found* that a broom had fallen out of the closet.

WHAT IS THE PAST PERFECT TENSE?

The **PAST PERFECT TENSE**, also called the **PLUPERFECT** in Latin,   1
is used to express an action completed in the past
before another action or event which
also occurred in the past.

> She *remembered* that she *had forgotten* her keys.
> simple past   past perfect
> 1   2

> Both actions 1 and 2 occurred in the past, but action 2
> preceded action 1. Therefore, action 2 is in the past perfect.
    10

IN ENGLISH

The past perfect is a verb phrase formed with the auxiliary
had + the past participle of the main verb: *I had eaten, he
had eaten*. In conversation, *had* is often shortened to *'d*
(She remembered that she*'d forgotten* her keys*)*.

Don't forget that verb tenses indicate the time that an
action occurs. Therefore, in order to show that actions
took place at different times, different tenses must be
used.

    20

> They *had moved* before school *opened* in the fall.
> past perfect   simple past
> 2   1

> Action 2 took place before action 1.

IN LATIN

The pluperfect is a tense formed with the perfect stem (see
p. 66) + the imperfect forms of **esse** *(to be):* **cantāv-** +
-eram → **cantāveram** *(I had sung)*, **cantāverās** *(you had
sung)*, **cantāverat** *(he had sung)*, etc.   30

As in English, a verb is put in the pluperfect in order to
stress that the action of that verb took place before the
action of a verb in either the perfect or the imperfect.
Observe the sequence of events expressed by the past tenses
in the following time-line:

VERB TENSE:	Pluperfect	Perfect or Imperfect	Present
	- 2	- 1	0
	x	x	x

TIME ACTION TAKES PLACE: 0 → now
-1 → before 0
-2 → before -1

- same verb tense → same moment in time

  *Niobe **was weeping** because Apollo **was killing** her sons.*
  Niobē **lacrimābat** quia Apollo fīliōs **necābat**.
  | |
  imperfect   imperfect
  -1   -1

  Two actions in the imperfect show that they took place at the same time in the past (before 0).

- different verb tenses → different times

  *Niobe **was weeping** because Apollo **had killed** her sons.*
  Niobē **lacrimābat** quia Apollo fīliōs **necāverat**.
  | |
  imperfect   pluperfect
  -1   -2

  The action in the pluperfect (point -2) occurred before the action in the imperfect (point -1).

✎ REVIEW

In the parentheses, number the verbs in *italics* according to where they are on the time-line on p. 69: -1 or -2.

- On the line below, indicate if the verb would be in the imperfect (I), perfect (P), or in the pluperfect (PP) in Latin.

1. Often the gods *came* to earth to see what the people *had done*.

   (-____)   (-____)

   _____   _____

2. The village people *had stoned* strangers; they *were* cruel.

   (-____)   (-____)

   _____   _____

3. Baucis and Philemon *were* kind; they *had welcomed* them.

   (-____)   (-____)

   _____   _____

4. Baucis *prepared* a meal; she *had stored* food.

   (-____)   (-____)

   _____   _____

22

WHAT IS THE FUTURE TENSE?

The FUTURE TENSE indicates that an action will take place   1
some time later than the present.

He *will see* you tomorrow.

IN ENGLISH

The future tense is expressed by a verb phrase formed with
the auxiliary *will* or *shall* + the dictionary form of the
main verb. In conversation, *shall* and *will* are often shortened to *'ll* (You *'ll* do it tomorrow).

Thisbe *will arrive* first.
Pyramus *will grieve* for her death.[1]   10

In practice the future time is often replaced with the verb
phrase "is going to" or the present tense.

Pyramus *is going to be* late.
Pyramus *will grieve* when he *sees* Thisbe's bloody veil.

future tense   present tense (future time)

IN LATIN

Unlike in English, you do not need an auxiliary verb to
show that an action will take place in the future. The
future tense is formed with the present stem (see p. 58) +   20
the future tense sign **-bi-** (or **-bu-**) for the 1st and 2nd conjugations or **-ē-** (or **-e-**) for the 3rd and 4th conjugations + personal endings similar to the present tense (see p. 57-9).
Consult your textbook for the complete four conjugations.

1st	cantā**bit**	*he/she/it will sing*
2nd	docē**bimus**	*we shall teach*
3rd	mitt**ēs**	*you will send*
4th	audi**ent**	*they will hear*

The use of the future tense in Latin corresponds to the use
of the future tense in English.   30

Thisbē prīma **adveniet**.

future

*Thisbe **will arrive** first.*

---

[1]Pyramus and Thisbe are young lovers whose marriage is prevented by their
parents. They agree to meet secretly and through mistakes kill themselves
thinking each has caused the death of the other.

Pȳramus mortem eius **dolēbit.**
|
future tense
*Pyramus **will grieve** for her death.*

N.B. While English occasionally uses the present tense after expressions such as *as soon as, when,* and *by the time,* which introduce an action that will take place in the future, Latin uses the future tense (see time-line p. 73).

*Pyramus **will grieve** when he **sees** Thisbe's scarf.*

future tense   present tense
(future time "as soon as he *will see* . . .")

Pȳramus **dolēbit** cum velāmen Thisbēs **vidēbit.**
| |
future tense   future tense

Latin is stricter than English in its use of tenses.

✎ REVIEW

Indicate the tense of the verb in *italics*: present (P) or future (F).
▪ Indicate the tense of the verb as it would be in a Latin sentence.

1. As soon as Pyramus and Thisbe *fall* in love, they *will want* to meet secretly.

In English:	P	F		P	F
In Latin:	P	F		P	F

2. When Thisbe *sees* the lion, she *will hide* in a cave.

In English:	P	F		P	F
In Latin:	P	F		P	F

3. Pyramus *will kill* himself after he *sees* Thisbe's bloody veil.

In English:	P	F		P	F
In Latin:	P	F		P	F

WHAT IS THE FUTURE PERFECT TENSE?

The FUTURE PERFECT TENSE is used to express an action which   1
will occur before another action in the future
or before a specific time in the future.

By the time we leave, he *will have finished.*

⎿————————⏌ ⎿——————⏌
 future event   future perfect
      2   1

Both actions 1 and 2 will occur at some future time, but
action 1 will be completed before action 2 takes place.
Therefore, action 1 is in the future perfect tense.

IN ENGLISH

The future perfect is a verb phrase formed with the auxil-   10
iary *will have* (or *shall have*) + the past participle of the
main verb (see p. 81): *I will have walked, she will have gone.*
In conversation *will* is shortened to *'ll* and, in some cases,
dropped altogether and *have* or *has* is shortened to *'ve* or *'s.*

I'll see you as soon as I *will [I'll] have finished.* [rarely used]
I'll see you as soon as I *have finished.* [rarely used]
I'll see you as soon as I*'ve finished.* [most common]

The future perfect is often used following expressions such
as *by then, by that time, by* + a date.

By the end of the month, he *will have graduated.*   20
By June, I *will have saved* enough to buy a car.

IN LATIN

The future perfect is a single word formed with the perfect
stem (see p. 66) + the future tense of **esse** *(to be)*: **cantāv-** +
-erō → **cantāverō** *(I will have sung),* **cantāveris** *(you will have
sung),* **cantāverit** *(he will have sung),* etc.

As in English, a verb is put in the future perfect in order
to stress that the action of that verb will take place before
the action of a verb in the future tense, or before a specific
future time. Observe the sequence of events expressed by   30
the future tenses in the following time-line:

VERB TENSE:	Present	Future perfect	Future
	0	1	2
	—x——————	x——————	x—

TIME ACTION TAKES PLACE: 0 → now
                                  1 → after 0 and before 2
                                  2 → after 0

*When Pyramus **arrives**, Thisbe **will have left**.*
present tense (future time implied)   future perfect
                    2   1

Cum Pȳramus **adveniet**, Thisbē **discesserit**.
        future tense   future perfect
              2   1

N.B. Remember that English often uses the present tense when a future time is implied (see p. 71). In the above example, the actions taking place at point 2 are in the present tense in English, but in the future tense in Latin. However, the actions taking place at point 1 are in the future perfect in both languages.

✎ REVIEW

Indicate the tense of the verb in *italics*: present (P), future (F), or future perfect (FP).
▪ Indicate the tense of the verb as it would be in a Latin sentence.

1. Pyramus *will kill* himself when he *sees* the bloody veil of Thisbe.

   | IN ENGLISH: | P | F | FP | P | F | FP |
   | IN LATIN: | P | F | FP | P | F | FP |

2. The blood of Pyramus *will have changed* the color of the fruit of the mulberry tree by the time Thisbe *returns*.

   | IN ENGLISH: | P | F | FP | P | F | FP |
   | IN LATIN: | P | F | FP | P | F | FP |

3. When Thisbe *comes back*, Pyramus already *will have killed* himself.

   | IN ENGLISH: | P | F | FP | P | F | FP |
   | IN LATIN: | P | F | FP | P | F | FP |

WHAT IS AN AUXILIARY VERB?

A verb is called an AUXILIARY VERB or HELPING VERB
when it helps another verb, called the MAIN VERB,
form one of its tenses. The auxiliary verb
plus a main verb form a VERB PHRASE.

verb phrase

Jupiter *was watching* the nymph.

auxiliary   main
verb   verb

IN ENGLISH

There are three auxiliary verbs, forms of *to be, to have,* and
to do, as well as a series of auxiliary words such as *will,*
would, may, must, can, could, and *used to* that are used to
change the tense and meaning of the main verb. Auxiliary
verbs and words serve many purposes:

- forms of *to be* — for the progressive of the present and
  past tenses (see *What is the Present Tense?*, p. 63; *What is
  the Past Tense?*, p. 65)

  Jupiter *is watching* the nymph.

  present progressive

  Apollo *was chasing* Daphne.

  past progressive

- forms of *to be* — for the passive voice (see *What is Meant
  by Active and Passive Voice?*, p. 89)

  The story *is read* by many students.

  present passive

  The play *was performed* by experienced actors.

  past passive

- forms of *to have* — for the perfect tenses (see *What is the
  Past Tense?*, p. 65; *What is the Past Perfect Tense?*, p. 69;
  What is the Future Perfect Tense?, p. 73)

  Latona *has called* her children.

  present perfect

Pan *had breathed* over the reeds.
|___|____|
past perfect

- forms of *to do* — for the emphatic forms of the present and past tenses (see *What is the Present Tense?*, p. 63; *What is the Past Tense?*, p. 65)

Jupiter *does like* to watch the nymph.
|___|____|
present emphatic

Pan *did make* a flute out of reeds.
|___|____|
past emphatic

- forms of *to do* — for questions and negative sentences (see *What are Declarative and Interrogative Sentences?*, p. 106)

Does Jupiter *watch* the nymph?
Apollo *does not chase* Daphne.

- *will* — to form the future tense (see *What is the Future Tense?*, p. 71)

Apollo **will** *chase* Daphne.

- *may* — to form ideas of possibility or probability (see *What is the Subjunctive Mood?*, p. 97)

The Argonauts *may come* tomorrow.

IN LATIN

Unlike English, Latin rarely uses verb phrases. Tenses and ideas that are expressed by a verb phrase in English are usually expressed by a simple verb in Latin.

Jupiter **is watching** *the nymph.*
|___|____|
IN ENGLISH: present progressive
IN LATIN: present → **spectat**

Latona **has called** *her children.*
|___|____|
IN ENGLISH: present perfect
IN LATIN: present perfect → **vocāvit**

The story **is read** *by many students.*
|___|____|
IN ENGLISH: present passive
IN LATIN: present passive → **legitur**

Jupiter **does love** *the nymphs.*
|___|____|
IN ENGLISH: present emphatic
IN LATIN: present → **amat**

REVIEW

Underline the verbs in the following paragraph.
■ Circle the verb phrases.

Phaethon demanded proof that his father was the sun god

Apollo. The boy asked permission to drive the chariot of the

sun across the sky for a day. Apollo was feeling sad because

his son had requested such a dangerous proof. When

Phaethon insisted, his father sorrowfully yoked the wild

horses of the sun chariot. The horses could feel the weak

hands on the reins and plunged wildly through the sky.

Alternately the earth was burned and was frozen. Finally

Jupiter hurled a thunderbolt at the chariot to save the earth,

but Phaethon was killed in the tragic fall.

CHAPTER

25

WHAT IS A PARTICIPLE?

A **PARTICIPLE** is a verb form which is part verb
and part adjective; it is called a **VERBAL ADJECTIVE.**
It can be used in one of two ways: with an auxiliary verb
to indicate certain tenses or as an adjective
to describe someone or something.

Pandora *has closed* the box.

auxiliary + participle → present perfect tense

The *closed* box now held only hope.

participle describing *box* → adjective

In English, there are two participles: the present participle
and the past participle. In Latin, there are three participles:
the present, the past, and the future participles.

PRESENT PARTICIPLE
IN ENGLISH

The present participle is easy to recognize because it is the
-ing form of the verb: work*ing,* study*ing,* danc*ing,* play*ing.*

The present participle has three functions:

1. as the main verb in a verb phrase with forms of the
   auxiliary *to be* in the progressive tenses (see pp. 63, 65)

   Theseus *is entering* the labyrinth.[1]

   present progressive of *to enter*

   Ariadne *was trying* to help Theseus.

   past progressive of *to try*

2. as an adjective describing a noun or pronoun (see
   p. 121)

   Theseus was a *daring* hero.

   describes the noun *hero*

   He was *daring.*

   describes the pronoun *he*

---

[1]Theseus went to Crete to kill the Minotaur, a creature half-man and half-
bull. The princess Ariadne gave him a ball of string to unwind so that he
could find his way out of the maze, called the labyrinth, where the
Minotaur was housed.

3. as an adjective introducing a participial phrase (see p. 103)

> Theseus, *seeing* the Minotaur, was not afraid.
> The entire phrase, *seeing the Minotaur*, works as an adjective modifying *Theseus*.

> No one saw Theseus *killing* the Minotaur.
> The entire phrase, *killing the Minotaur*, works as an adjective modifying *Theseus*.

IN LATIN

The present participle is called the **PRESENT ACTIVE PARTICIPLE**, "active" because it is always active in meaning (see *What is Meant by Active and Passive Voice?*, p. 89). It is formed with the present stem of the verb (see p. 58) + **-ns** (nom. sing.), **-ntis** (gen. sing.) and acts as an adjective of the 3ʳᵈ declension, Group B (see pp. 123-4). As an adjective, it must agree in case, gender, and number with the noun or pronoun modified (see *What is an Adjective?*, p. 120). Here is an example for each of the four conjugations:

1ᵀ CONJUGATION	cantāns, cantantis	*singing*
2ᴺᴰ CONJUGATION	docēns, docentis	*teaching*
3ᴿᴰ CONJUGATION	mittēns, mittentis	*sending*
3ᴿᴰ -io	capiēns, capientis	*taking*
4ᵀᴴ CONJUGATION	audiēns, audientis	*hearing*

Unlike in English where the present participle can be part of a verb phrase, the present active participle in Latin can only function as an adjective. The present active participle is used in one of two ways.

1. as a descriptive adjective (see p. 121)

> *Theseus was a **daring** hero.*
> 1. NOUN MODIFIED: hero
> 2. CASE: *Hero* is a predicate word → nominative
> 3. GENDER & NUMBER: **Hēros** *(hero)* is masculine singular.
> Thēseus erat hēros **audēns**.
> |
>   present active participle
>   nom. masc. sing.

> *Theseus saw the **burning** palace.*
> 1. NOUN MODIFIED: palace
> 2. CASE: *Palace* is a direct object → accusative
> 3. GENDER & NUMBER: **Rēgia** *(palace)* is feminine singular.
> Thēseus rēgiam **conflagrantem** vīdit.
> |
>   present active participle
>   acc. fem. sing.

2. as an adjective introducing a participial phrase (see p. 103)

*Theseus, **seeing** the Minotaur, was not afraid.*
1. NOUN MODIFIED: Theseus
2. CASE: *Theseus* is a subject → nominative
3. GENDER & NUMBER: **Theseus** is masculine singular.

Thēseus Mīnōtaurum **vidēns** nōn timēbat.
present active participle
nom. masc. sing.

*No one saw Theseus **killing** the Minotaur.*
1. NOUN MODIFIED: Theseus
2. CASE: *Theseus* is a direct object → accusative
3. GENDER & NUMBER: **Theseus** is masculine singular.

Nēmo Thēseum Mīnōtaurum **necantem** vīdit.
present active participle
acc. masc. sing.

N.B. — Never assume that an English word ending in *-ing* will be translated by a Latin present active participle.

1. It could be a progressive form of an English verb whose Latin equivalent is a simple verb form.

*Orpheus **is singing**.*[1]
present progressive
Orpheus **cantat**.
present (see p. 63)

*The animals **were listening**.*
past progressive
Animālia **audiēbant**.
imperfect (see p. 65)

*Eurydice **will be coming** soon.*
future progressive
Eurydice **veniet**.
future (see p. 71)

2. It could be a verbal noun (see *What is a Gerund?*, p. 86).

*The art of **singing** is difficult .*
noun from the verb *to sing*
Ars **cantandī** difficilis est.
gerund

---

[1]At her marriage to the famous singer Orpheus, Eurydice was bitten by a snake and died. The king of the Underworld allowed her to follow Orpheus back to Earth, on the condition that Orpheus not look back at her. Unfortunately, he did and Eurydice disappeared forever.

Consult the chart summarizing the various English *-ing* forms and their Latin equivalents on p. 88.

PAST PARTICIPLE
IN ENGLISH

The past participle is the form of the verb that follows *I have*: I have *spoken*, I have *written*, I have *walked*. The past participle has three functions: 120

1. as part of a verb phrase

- as the main verb with forms of the auxiliary verb *to have* to form the perfect tenses of the active voice (see *What is the Past Tense?*, p. 65 and *What is the Past Perfect Tense?*, p. 69)

    The mighty city of Troy *has fallen*.[1]

    present perfect of *to fall*

    Many Trojan heroes *had died*. 130

    past perfect of *to die*

- as the main verb with forms of the auxiliary verb *to be* to form the present and past tenses of the passive voice (see *Perfect tenses in the passive voice*, p. 91)

    Many Trojan heroes *are killed* in the war.

    present passive of *to kill*

    The Trojan horse *was dragged* into the city.

    past passive of *to drag* 140

2. as an adjective to describe a noun (see p. 121)

    The *captured* city was burned by the Greeks.

    describes the noun *city*

    Hecuba buried her *murdered* sons.

    describes the noun *sons*

3. as an adjective introducing a participial phrase (p. 103)

    Troy, *captured* by the Greeks, was burned.

    The entire phrase, *captured by the Greeks*, works as an adjective modifying *Troy*. 150

    The Trojan women, *dragged* by the hair, were carried off.

    The entire phrase, *dragged by the hair*, works as an adjective modifying *Trojan women*.

---

[1]The Trojan War was fought by the Greeks to recover the beautiful Queen Helen who had been abducted by Paris, the son of the king of Troy.

IN LATIN

The past participle is called the **PERFECT PASSIVE PARTICIPLE,** "passive" because it is always passive in meaning. It is listed as the fourth principal part of the verb ending in **-us, -a, -um** (see p. 52) and acts as an adjective of the 1ˢᵗ and 2ⁿᵈ declension, Group A (see pp. 122-3). As an adjective, it must agree in case, gender, and number with the noun or pronoun modified (see *What is an Adjective?*, p. 120). Here is an example for each of the four conjugations:

1ˢᵀ CONJUGATION	cantātus, -a, -um	*having been sung*
2ᴺᴰ CONJUGATION	doctus, -a, -um	*having been taught*
3ᴿᴰ CONJUGATION	missus, -a, -um	*having been sent*
3ᴿᴰ -io	captus, -a, -um	*having been taken*
4ᵀᴴ CONJUGATION	audītus, -a, -um	*having been heard*

The perfect passive participle has three major functions:

1. as the main verb with forms of the auxiliary **esse** (*to be*) to form the perfect tenses of the passive voice (see p. 91)

*Many Trojan heroes have been **killed** in the war.*
1. NOUN MODIFIED: heroes
2. CASE: *Heroes* is a subject → nominative
3. GENDER & NUMBER: **Hērōēs** *(heroes)* is masculine plural.

Multī hērōēs Trōiānī in bellō **necātī** sunt.
⌐‾‾‾‾‾‾‾‾‾‾‾‾‾‾‾‾‾‾‾‾‾¬
perfect passive participle + **sunt**
nom. masc. pl.

*The city of Troy has been **burned** by the Greeks.*
1. NOUN MODIFIED: city
2. CASE: *City* is a subject → nominative
3. GENDER & NUMBER: **Urbs** *(city)* is feminine singular.

Urbs Trōia ā Graecīs **incensa** est.
⌐‾‾‾‾‾‾‾‾‾¬
perfect passive participle + **est**
nom. fem. sing.

2. as an adjective to describe a noun (see p. 121)

*The Greeks burned the **captured** city.*
1. NOUN MODIFIED: city
2. CASE: *City* is a direct object → accusative
3. GENDER & NUMBER: **Urbem** *(city)* is feminine singular.

Graecī urbem **captam** incendērunt.
|
perfect passive participle
acc. fem. sing.

*Hecuba buried her **murdered** sons.*
1. NOUN MODIFIED: sons
2. CASE: *Sons* is a direct object → accusative
3. GENDER & NUMBER: **Fīliōs** *(sons)* is masculine plural.

Hecuba fīliōs **necātōs** sepelīvit.
|
perfect passive participle
acc. masc. pl.

160

170

180

190

3. as an adjective introducing a participial phrase (see p. 103)

(see p. 103)

participial phrase   200

Driven by wind, the Greek ships came to Troy.
1. NOUN MODIFIED: ships
2. CASE: *Ships* is a subject → nominative
3. GENDER & NUMBER: **Nāvēs** *(ships)* is feminine plural.

Pulsae ventō nāvēs Graecae Trōiam advēnērunt.

perfect passive participle
nom. fem. pl.

participial phrase

*The Trojans saw the horse **abandoned** by the Greeks.*
1. NOUN MODIFIED: horse   210
2. CASE: *Horse* is a direct object → accusative
3. GENDER & NUMBER: **Equum** *(horse)* is masculine singular.

Troiānī equum ā Graecīs **relictum** vīdērunt.

perfect passive participle
acc. masc. sing.

4. within an ablative absolute

The **ABLATIVE ABSOLUTE** construction is very common in
Latin: it consists of two words in the ablative case, often
a noun and a perfect passive participle. Although grammatically independent (hence the term "absolute") of the   220
subject or the object of the main clause (see pp. 103-4), it
is logically connected to explain the circumstances sur-
rounding the action of the main verb.

(see pp. 103-4)

ablative absolute

Mīnōtaurō **necātō**, Theseus ab īnsulā discessit.

perfect passive participle
modifying **Mīnōtaurō**
both in ablative masculine singular

*The Minotaur **having been killed**, Theseus left the island.*
*After the Minotaur **had been killed**, Theseus left the island.*   230

N. B. Keep in mind that the equivalent of English active
tenses formed with the auxiliary verb *have* + past participle
do not use participles in Latin, but correspond to simple
tenses in Latin.

*I **have seen** the beautiful city of Troy.*

present perfect

Urbem Trōiam pulchram **vīdī**.

perfect (see p. 66)   240

(see p. 66)

FUTURE PARTICIPLES
IN ENGLISH
There are no future participle verb forms. However, there are English constructions that require the use of future participles in Latin. There are two English constructions most commonly associated with the future participles:

- "to be about to do something"→ the future active participle

  He is *about to do* his homework.

- "something is about to be done" stressing the obligation or necessity to perform an act → the future passive participle

  He has homework *to be done.*

IN LATIN
There are two future participles, active and passive (see *What is Meant by Active and Passive Voice?*, p. 89). They are **VERBAL ADJECTIVES**; i.e., verb forms used as adjectives. Let us consider them separately since each has different uses.

FUTURE ACTIVE PARTICIPLE
The **FUTURE ACTIVE PARTICIPLE** is an adjective of the 1ˢᵗ and 2ⁿᵈ declension declined like Group A (see pp. 122-3), formed with the stem of the fourth principal part of the verb (see pp. 51, 52) + -ūrus, -ūra, -ūrum.

ventūrus, -a, -um	*about to come*
futūrus, -a, -um	*about to be*

As an adjective, it must agree in case, gender, and number with the noun or pronoun modified (see *What is an Adjective?*, p. 120).

*The gladiators **about to die** saluted the emperor.*
Gladiātōrēs **moritūrī** imperātōrem salūtāvērunt.
       |
    future active participle
    nom. masc. pl. modifying **gladiātōrēs** *(gladiators)*

The future active participle is used to form the future infinitive **futūrus** (-a, -um) **esse** (see p. 54).

FUTURE PASSIVE PARTICIPLE
The **FUTURE PASSIVE PARTICIPLE**, also called the **GERUNDIVE**, is an adjective of the 1ˢᵗ and 2ⁿᵈ declension declined like Group A (see pp. 122-3) formed with the present stem of the verb (see p. 58) + -ndus, -nda, -ndum.

cantandus, -a, -um	*about to be sung*
legendus, -a, -um	*about to be read*

As an adjective, it must agree in case, gender, and number with the noun or pronoun modified (see *What is an Adjective?*, p. 120).

Librum **legendum** habeō.

> future passive participle (gerundive)
> acc. masc. sing. modifying **librum**

*I have a book **to be read**.*
*I have a book which **should be read**.* [obligation implied]

The future passive participle (the gerundive) is often used with a form of **esse** as a verb phrase expressing an obligation or necessity. This usage is called the **PASSIVE PERIPHRASTIC.**

290

Hic liber tibi **legendus est**.

> passive periphrastic
> fut. pass. part. (gerundive) + **est**
> nom. sing. masc. modifying **liber**

*This book **must be read** by you.*

 REVIEW

Underline the participles in the sentences below.

- Circle whether each participle is used as an adjective (A) or as part of a verb phrase (VP).

1. Theseus, growing up, did not know that his father was king of Athens.	A	VP
2. Theseus found the sword and sandals which had been left by his father.	A	VP
3. Desiring to meet his father, Theseus set out for Athens.	A	VP
4. Youths and maidens were chosen by lot to go to Crete.	A	VP
5. Theseus volunteered to go with the chosen youths.	A	VP

WHAT IS A GERUND?

A GERUND is a verb form which is part verb and part noun; it is called a VERBAL NOUN.

Studying is hard work.

gerund → verbal noun, subject of *is*

IN ENGLISH

The gerund is composed of the dictionary form of the verb + -*ing*: talk*ing*, walk*ing*. It can function in a sentence in almost any way that a noun can: as a subject, as an object of a verb or of a preposition.

Singing is an art.

noun from the verb *to sing*
subject of *is*

Do you enjoy *singing*?

noun from the verb *to sing*
direct object of verb *to enjoy*

The art of *singing* is difficult.

noun from the verb *to sing*
object of the preposition *of*

N.B. — Since the English -*ing* form of the verb can be part of a verb phrase, a verbal adjective (present participle), or a verbal noun (gerund), it is important to distinguish among these three uses in order to choose the correct Latin equivalent (see chart p. 88).

Maria *is singing*.

verb phrase
progressive present tense

He was a *singing* musician.

verbal adjective
present participle

Singing is an art.

gerund

IN LATIN

The gerund is a neuter noun of the 2ⁿᵈ declension formed from the present stem of the verb (see p. 58) + -ndī (gen.), -ndō (dat.), -ndum (acc.), -ndō (abl.).

GENITIVE	cantandī	*singing*	docendī	*teaching*
DATIVE	cantandō		docendō	
ACCUSATIVE	cantandum		docendum	
ABLATIVE	cantandō		docendō	

The gerund is primarily used in the genitive, dative and ablative cases.

Ars **cantandī** difficilis est.
     |
     genitive
*The art **of singing** is difficult.*
          |
          object of preposition *of*

Amāre discit **amandō**.
               |
               ablative
*He learns to love **by loving**.*
                    |
                    object of preposition *by*

The use of the gerund in the accusative is primarily with the preposition **ad** *(to)* to indicate purpose.

Athēnās **ad vīvendum** bene it.
*He goes to Athens **to live** well [the good life].*

When a verbal noun functions as a subject or as a direct object, Latin does not use the gerund but the infinitive of the verb (notice that there is no nominative form above).

Cantāre est ars.
     |
infinitive
Singing [to sing] is an art.
     |
subject

Amāsne **cantāre**?
          |
          infinitive
*Do you like **singing [to sing]**?*
               |
               direct object

SUMMARY

Here is a reference chart summarizing the various English -*ing* forms and their Latin equivalents.

English -*ING*	Latin Equivalent
Verb phrase auxiliary + present ⟶ ex. *is singing* *was singing* *will be singing*	various simple tenses present past future
Adjective present participle ⟶ ex. *singing* musician	present active participle (present stem + -**ns**, -**ntis**[1])
Noun (gerund) subject of a verb ⟶ ex. *Singing* is an art. direct object of a verb ⟶ ex. Do you like *singing?* other functions ⟶ ex. *of, to,* or *by singing*	infinitive infinitive gerund (present stem + -**ndī**, -**ndum**, -**ndō**[1])

80

90

✎ REVIEW

Circle the -*ing* word in the sentences below.
- Circle whether the -*ing* word is a gerund (G), a participle (P), or part of a verb phrase (VP).

1. Hoping to kill the Minotaur,
   Theseus went to Crete.   G   P   VP

2. Theseus devoted himself to training
   for the encounter with the Minotaur.   G   P   VP

3. Theseus was always training himself
   as a wrestler.   G   P   VP

4. The youths had little hope of escaping.   G   P   VP

5. By dancing with the bull,
   Theseus entertained the Cretans.   G   P   VP

[1]Except for 3ʳᵈ -**iō** and 4ᵗʰ conjugations which add an -i to the stem.

WHAT IS MEANT BY ACTIVE
AND PASSIVE VOICE?

VOICE in the grammatical sense refers to the relationship
between the verb and its subject. There are two voices,
the ACTIVE VOICE and the PASSIVE VOICE.

ACTIVE VOICE — A sentence is said to be in the active voice
when the subject is the performer of the action of the
verb. The direct object is the receiver of the action (see
What is a Subject?, p. 30 and *What are Objects?*, p. 36). In
this instance, the verb is called an ACTIVE VERB.

> The king touches the food.[1]
> subject verb direct object

The subject, *the king,* performs the action of the verb *(he is
doing the touching),* and the direct object, *the food,* is the
receiver of the action.

PASSIVE VOICE — A sentence is said to be in the passive
voice when the subject is the receiver of the action of the
verb. The performer of the action, if it is mentioned, is
introduced by the word "by" and is called the AGENT. In
this instance, the verb is called a PASSIVE VERB.

> The food is touched by the king.
> subject verb agent

The subject, *the food,* is not the performer of the action of
the verb; it is the receiver of the action *(it is being touched).*
The performer of the action, *the king,* is the agent.

IN ENGLISH

The passive voice is expressed by a form of the verb *to be*
conjugated in the appropriate tense + the past participle of
the main verb (see *What is a Participle?*, p. 78). The tense of
the passive sentence is indicated by the tense of *to be.*

> The food *is touched* by the king.
> present passive

---

[1]King Midas received the golden touch from a god. At first when everything
turned to gold, the gift seemed a blessing; however, when the king tried to
eat and drink, it became a curse.

The food *was touched* by the king.

past passive

The food *will be touched* by the king.

future passive

N.B. Do not confuse the verb phrase *to be* + the past participle of the verb which forms the passive voice (see examples above) and the verb phrase *to be* + the present participle of the verb (see p. 78) which forms the active voice of the progressive tenses (see examples below).

The king *is touching* the food.

present progressive active

The king *was touching* the food.

past progressive active

IN LATIN

Unlike in English, not all passive verbs in Latin are expressed with an auxiliary verb. We shall divide passive verbs according to the way they are formed: without an auxiliary verb → the present, imperfect, and future tenses, or with an auxiliary verb → the perfect tenses.

PRESENT, IMPERFECT AND FUTURE TENSES IN THE PASSIVE VOICE

The present, imperfect, and future passive tenses are expressed by special passive endings, without an auxiliary verb. These endings, the same for the three tenses, are added to the present stem (see p. 58), with the appropriate tense signs for the imperfect (see p. 65) and the future (see p. 71).

PERSON	SINGULAR		PLURAL	
1st	*I*	-r	*we*	-mur
2nd	*you*	-ris	*you*	-minī
3rd	*he/she/it*	-tur	*they*	-ntur

PRESENT PASSIVE: present stem + passive endings

Cibus ā rēge **tangitur.**
*The food **is touched** by the king.*

IMPERFECT PASSIVE: present stem + -bā- + passive endings

Cibus ā rēge **tangēbātur.**
*The food **was touched** by the king.*

FUTURE PASSIVE: present stem + -bi- or -ē- + passive endings

Cibus ā rēge **tangētur.**
*The food **will be touched** by the king.*

Perfect Tenses in the Passive Voice

The perfect, past perfect, and future perfect passive tenses require the use of an auxiliary verb. They are formed with the perfect passive participle (the fourth principal part, see p. 51) + a form of **esse** *(to be)* conjugated in the appropriate tense to form a verb phrase. The tense of the auxiliary **esse** affects the tense of the passive sentence. As adjectives, perfect passive participles (p. 82) must agree with the nouns they modify in case (always nominative subjects), gender, and number (see *What is an Adjective?*, p. 120).

PERFECT PASSIVE: perfect passive participle + present tense of **esse**

Cibus **tactus est.**
 | |_____|
nom.   perfect passive
masc. sing.
*The food **has been touched**.*

PAST PERFECT (PLUPERFECT) PASSIVE: perfect passive participle + imperfect tense of **esse**

Cibus **tactus erat.**
*The food **had been touched**.*

FUTURE PERFECT PASSIVE: perfect passive participle + future tense of **esse**

Cibus **tactus erit.**
*The food **will have been touched**.*

Passive endings are easily distinguished from the active endings.

Cibus ā rēge **tangitur.**	Rex cibum **tangit.**
present passive	present active
*The food **is touched** by the king.*	*The king **touches** the food.*

The Agent

In Latin the agent, i.e., the person or thing doing the action of the verb, is expressed by the ablative case. When the agent is a person, the ablative is preceded by the preposition **ā** (**ab** before a vowel). This construction is called ABLATIVE OF AGENT.

ā rēge   *by the king*

When the agent is a thing, there is no preposition. This construction is called ABLATIVE OF MEANS.

ventō   *by the wind*

DEPONENT VERBS

There is a type of verb particular to Latin which you must learn to recognize. These verbs are conjugated like passive verbs, but they have active meanings. They are called DEPO-NENT VERBS from the Latin verb **dēpōnere**, *to lay aside*, because they have "laid aside" their passive meaning. Your Latin textbook will present the complete conjugation of these verbs which have only three principal parts, e.g. **loquor, loquī, locūtus sum** *(to speak)*.

Note the difference in endings between two verbs related to speech: **dīcit** *(he says)*, an active verb in the present tense; **loquitur** *(he speaks)*, a deponent verb in the present tense.

> **Dīcit** mē esse amīcum.
> *He says that I am his friend.*
>
> **Loquitur** cum amīcō.
> *He speaks with his friend.*

Your Latin textbook will present the complete conjugation of deponent verbs.

✎ REVIEW

Underline the verb or the verb phrase in the sentences below.
■ Circle whether each verb is active (A) or passive (P).

1. The leaves of the maple tree were falling.   A   P

2. The leaves were raked by the boy
   and his father.   A   P

3. Did you carry the gifts for the goddess
   into the temple?   A   P

4. Were the gifts for the goddess given freely?   A   P

5. Has the signal been given for the race?   A   P

6. Will the news of the winner
   be announced today?   A   P

28

WHAT IS MEANT BY MOOD?

MOOD in the grammatical sense applies to verbs
and indicates the attitude of the speaker
toward what he or she is saying or doing.

1

Different moods serve different purposes. For example,
verb forms that state a fact belong to one mood *(you are
studying, you studied)*, and verb forms that give orders
belong to another mood *(Study!)*. Some moods have multiple tenses while others have only one tense.

You should recognize the names of the moods so that
you will know what your Latin textbook is referring to
when it uses these terms. You will learn when to use the
various moods as you learn verbs and their tenses.

10

IN ENGLISH

Verbs can be in one of three moods.

1. The INDICATIVE MOOD is used to state the action of the
   verb, that is, to *indicate* facts. This is the most common
   mood, and most of the verb forms that you use in
   everyday conversation belong to the indicative mood.
   The majority of the tenses studied in this handbook
   belong to the indicative mood: for example, the present
   tense (see p. 63), the past tense (see p. 65), and the
   future tense (see p. 71).

20

   Medea *is* Jason's helper.[1]
   present indicative

   Jason *found* the Golden Fleece.
   past indicative

   Will Jason always *love* Medea?
   future indicative

30

2. The IMPERATIVE MOOD is used to give commands or orders
   (see p. 95). This mood is not divided into tenses.

   Jason, *find* the Golden Fleece!
   Medea, *help* Jason!

---

[1]Jason went to the land of Colchis to bring back the Golden Fleece. Medea,
the daughter of the king of Colchis, aided him, and he brought her back as
his bride. Eventually, however, he left her for another woman.

3. The **SUBJUNCTIVE MOOD** is used to express an action that is not really occurring. It is the language of wish, possibility, condition, and other vague situations (see p. 97).

> Medea wishes that Jason *were* her husband.
> If Medea *were* loyal, she would not betray her father.
> The king insists that Jason *find* the Golden Fleece.

IN LATIN

The Latin language identifies the same three moods.

1. The **INDICATIVE MOOD,** as in English, is the most common and most of the tenses you will learn belong to this mood.

> *My sister **is coming**.*
> Soror mea **venit**.
> |
>   present indicative

2. The **IMPERATIVE MOOD,** as in English, is used to express commands.

> *Sister, **come** with me.*
> Soror, **venī** mēcum.
> |
>   imperative

3. The **SUBJUNCTIVE MOOD** is used much more frequently in Latin than in English. Unlike in English, the subjunctive mood in Latin is divided into four tenses. Textbooks will use the term "present subjunctive" to distinguish it from the "present indicative."

> *My sister **may come** with us.*
> Soror mea nōbīscum **veniat**.
> |
>   present subjunctive

When there is no reference to mood, the verb belongs to the most common mood, the indicative.

29

WHAT IS THE IMPERATIVE MOOD?

The IMPERATIVE is the mood of the verb used to give
a person or persons a command.
The AFFIRMATIVE IMPERATIVE is an order to do something.
Come here!

The NEGATIVE IMPERATIVE is an order not to do something.
Do not [don't] come here!

IN ENGLISH

There are two forms of commands, depending on who is
told to do, or not to do, something. Both types of command use the dictionary form of the verb.

1. "YOU" COMMAND — When an order is given to one or
   more persons, the dictionary form of the verb is used.

AFFIRMATIVE IMPERATIVE	NEGATIVE IMPERATIVE
Medea, *come* with me!	Medea, *do not come* with me!
Sailors, *load* the ship!	Sailors, *do not load* the ship!

   In these sentences, neither Medea nor the sailors is the
   subject of the verb; the speaker is merely calling out
   their names, but rather the subject is "you" which is
   understood.

2. "LET" COMMAND — When an order is given to oneself as
   well as to others, the word "let" (*let's* is a contraction of
   let us) is used + the dictionary form of the verb.

AFFIRMATIVE IMPERATIVE	NEGATIVE IMPERATIVE
Let's leave!	*Let's not leave!*
Let them *die!*	*Let* them *not die!*

IN LATIN

As in English, there are "you" and "we" affirmative and
negative commands. However, different moods and different forms are used.

AFFIRMATIVE COMMANDS

1. "YOU" COMMANDS — Only the 2nd person affirmative commands use a special form of the verb called the IMPERATIVE
   MOOD. The singular form is the present stem and the plural form is the present stem + -**te**.

   > Mēdēa, **venī** mēcum. [addressing one person]
   > *Medea, **come** with me.*

Argonautae, **venīte** mēcum. [addressing more than one person]
*Argonauts, **come** with me.*[1]

2. **"LET" COMMANDS** — These forms use either the 1ˢᵗ or 3ʳᵈ person of the present subjunctive (see *What is the Subjunctive Mood?*, p. 97).

Vīvāmus!
Let us live!

Vīvat!
Let him live!

NEGATIVE COMMANDS

1. **"YOU" COMMANDS** — These forms are expressed by the verb meaning "to be unwilling": **nōlī** (sing.) and **nōlīte** (pl.) + the infinitive of the verb.

Mēdēa, **nōlī venīre** mēcum.
*Medea, **don't come** with me.*

Argonautae, **nōlīte venīre** mēcum.
*Argonauts, **don't come** with me.*

2. **"LET" COMMANDS** — These forms are expressed by the negative **nē** + 1ˢᵗ or 3ʳᵈ person of the present subjunctive.

Nē vīvat!
Let him not live!

Consult your Latin textbook for all imperative forms of active and passive verbs, as well as for deponent verbs.

✎ REVIEW

Circle the verb and negatives in the following sentences.
- Indicate whether the Latin verb should be singular (S) or plural (P).

1. Jason, sow the teeth of the dragon!	S	P
2. Sailors, go on board the ship!	S	P
3. Let Medea obey her father!	S	P
4. Let us not forget our duty!	S	P
5. Medea, do not kill your brother!	S	P

---

[1]The Argonauts are sailors on the ship, the Argo, who sailed with Jason in search of the Golden Fleece.

WHAT IS THE SUBJUNCTIVE MOOD?

The **SUBJUNCTIVE** is a mood used to express a wish,
hope, uncertainty or other similar attitudes
toward a fact or an idea.

> I wish he *were* here.
> | |
>   verb of subjunctive
>   wishing

> The teacher insisted that the homework *be* neat.
> | |
>   verb of   subjunctive
>   attitude

IN ENGLISH

The subjunctive verb form is difficult to recognize because
it is spelled like other tenses of the verb: the dictionary
form or the simple past tense.

INDICATIVE	SUBJUNCTIVE
He *reads* a lot.	The course requires that he *read* a lot.
present indicative of *to read*	subjunctive (same as dictionary form)
I *am* in Detroit right now.	I wish that I *were* in Rome.
present indicative *to be*	subjunctive (same as past tense)

The subjunctive occurs most commonly in three kinds of
sentences.

1. in contrary-to-fact statements (see pp. 117-8)

>   contrary-to-fact (person speaking is not in Europe)
> If I *were* in Europe now, I would go to Rome.
> |
> subjunctive

>   contrary-to fact (he is not in shape)
> John would run faster, if he *were* in shape.
> |
>   subjunctive

2. in statements expressing a wish

> I wish I *were* in Europe right now.
> |
>   subjunctive

I wish she *were* my teacher.
|
subjunctive

3. in clauses (see p. 103-4) following verbs that ask, urge, demand, request or express necessity

I recommend that he *take* the course.
|_____|　　　　|
urge　　subjunctive (instead of indicative *takes*)

I move that the officers *be* elected annually.
|___|　　　　|
ask　　subjunctive (instead of indicative *are elected*)

These are just a few examples to show that English has the subjunctive form, but it is not used as frequently as it is used in Latin.

IN LATIN

The subjunctive mood has four tenses: the present, imperfect, perfect, and past perfect, each one having an active and a passive voice. Consult your textbook for the subjunctive forms of the four conjugations.

The subjunctive mood is often used in Latin. Below you will find various uses of the Latin subjunctive, and a list of some of the chapters of this handbook where they are discussed.

- in contrary-to-fact statements (see *What are Conditional Sentences?*, p. 117)

    *If I **were** in Europe, I would go to Rome.*
    Sī in Eurōpā **essem**, Rōmam īrem.

- in the clause following verbs of asking, etc. (see *What is Meant by Direct and Indirect Questions?*, p. 113)

    *Jason asked where the fleece **was**.*
    Jāson rogāvit ubi vellus **esset**.

- to give orders (see *What is the Imperative Mood?*, p. 95)

    Let us live and let us love.
    Vīvāmus et **amēmus**.

- to express a wish or following a verb of wishing

    *I wished that my father **were** still alive.*
    Voluī ut pater meus etiam vīvus **esset**.

There are many other uses of the subjunctive in Latin, and we refer you to the explanations and examples in your Latin textbook.

WHAT IS A CONJUNCTION?

A **CONJUNCTION** is a word that links two
or more words or groups of words.

> Jason *and* Medea fled from her father.
> Neither Jason *nor* Medea remained in Colchis.
> Medea loved Jason, *until* he left her.

IN ENGLISH

There are two kinds of conjunctions: coordinating and
subordinating.

- a **COORDINATING CONJUNCTION** joins words, phrases (groups
  of words without a verb), and clauses (groups of words
  with a verb) that are equal; it *coordinates* elements of
  equal rank. The major coordinating conjunctions are
  and, but, or, nor, for, and *yet.*

  good *or* evil
    | |
  word   word

  over the river *and* through the trees
  └────┬────┘   └──────┬──────┘
     phrase   phrase

  The sea was rough, *but* the lovers were happy.
  └──────┬──────┘   └──────┬──────┘
      clause   clause

  In the last example, each of the two clauses, "the sea
  was rough" and "the lovers were happy," expresses a
  complete thought; therefore, each clause could stand
  alone. When a clause expresses a complete thought and
  can stand alone, it is called a **MAIN CLAUSE**. In the above
  sentence, the coordinating conjunction *but* links two
  clauses of each rank, two main clauses.

- a **SUBORDINATING CONJUNCTION** joins a dependent clause to
  a main clause; it *subordinates* one clause to another. A
  DEPENDENT CLAUSE does not express a complete thought;
  therefore, it cannot stand alone. There are various types
  of dependent clauses. A clause introduced by a subordinating conjunction is called a **SUBORDINATE CLAUSE**.
  Typical subordinating conjunctions are *before, after,
  since, until, although, because, if, unless, so that, while,
  that,* and *when.*

40

main clause   subordinate clause

The lovers were happy, *until* Jason wanted a new wife.

subordinating
conjunction

subordinate clause   main clause

Although the sea was rough, the lovers were happy.

subordinating
conjunction

main clause   subordinate clause

50

Medea was angry *because* Jason had left her.

subordinating
conjunction

The subordinating conjunction changes a main clause into a subordinate clause which may come either at the end or the beginning of the sentence.

IN LATIN

Conjunctions must be memorized as vocabulary items. They never change their form, i.e., they do not have case, number, or gender: **et** *(and)*, **sed** *(but)*, **aut** *(or)*, **quod** *(because)*, **sī** *(if)*, **cum** *(when)*, **ubi** *(where)*, etc.

60

Some subordinating conjunctions require the use of the indicative mood for the verb which follows; others require the use of the subjunctive mood. Some can be followed by either mood, depending on the meaning of the sentence. When you learn a new conjunction, be sure to memorize what mood it requires.

SUBORDINATING CONJUNCTION OR PREPOSITION?

(see *What is a Preposition?*, p. 18)

70

It is important that you distinguish between a word functioning as a subordinating conjunction and one functioning as a preposition. Occasionally the same word can be used in English, but two different words must be used in Latin. For example, in English, *before* can be used as a subordinating conjunction or as a preposition. In Latin, however, *before* as a subordinating conjunction is **antequam**, but *before* as a preposition is **ante** or **prō**.

We can distinguish between a subordinating conjunction and a preposition by determining if the word in question

80

introduces a subordinate clause or a prepositional phrase (see pp. 99, 18).

prepositional phrase

*Medea loved Jason **before** their departure.*

preposition   object of preposition

Mēdēa Iāsonem amābat **ante** discessum.

preposition object of preposition

subordinate clause

*Medea loved Jason **before** he sought another woman.*   90

subject verb   object
subordinating
conjunction

Mēdēa Iāsonem amābat **antequam** aliam fēminam petīvit.

subordinating   object   verb
conjunction

prepositional phrase

After the voyage, Jason and Medea lived in Greece.

preposition   object of preposition   100

Post nāvigātiōnem, Iāson et Mēdēa in Graeciā habitābant.

preposition   object of preposition

subordinate clause

After the voyage was over, Jason and Medea lived in Greece.

subordinating subject verb
conjunction

Postquam nāvigātio fīnīta est, Iāson et Mēdēa in Graeciā habitābant.

subordinating   subject   verb
conjunction   110

✎ REVIEW

Circle whether the word in *italics* is a preposition (P) or a subordinating conjunction (SC).

1. Theseus became king *after* he returned to Athens.   P   SC

2. *Because* he befriended Oedipus, his fame increased.   P   SC

3. *After* his father's death, Theseus ruled many years.   P   SC

4. *Before* him stretched many years of service.   P   SC

5. *Because of* his wisdom, he became a famous king.   P   SC

6. *Before* he became king, Theseus had many adventures.   P   SC

CHAPTER

32

WHAT ARE SENTENCES, PHRASES, AND CLAUSES?

WHAT IS A SENTENCE?

A SENTENCE is the expression of a thought usually consisting at least of a subject (see *What is a Subject?*, p. 30) and a verb (see *What is a Verb?*, p. 48).

> Atalanta lost.
> subject   verb

> The people were cheering.
> subject   verb phrase

> How did Hippomenes win?[1]
> subject
> verb phrase

Depending on the verb, a sentence may also have direct and indirect objects (see *What are Objects?*, p. 36).

> Atalanta lost the race.
> subject   verb   direct object

> The king gave him the reward.
> subject   verb   indirect   direct
> object   object

In addition, a sentence may include various kinds of modifiers: adjectives (see *What is an Adjective?*, p. 120), adverbs (see *What is an Adverb?*, p. 141), and phrases (see below).

WHAT IS A PHRASE?

A PHRASE is a group of two or more words expressing a thought, but without a subject or a conjugated verb. The various phrases are identified by the type of word beginning the phrase.

PREPOSITIONAL PHRASE: a preposition + object of preposition

> Spectators cheered *along* the way.
> preposition

> Hippomenes was exalted *after* the race.

> Atalanta was diverted *towards* the end.

---

[1]All the young men who wanted to marry Atalanta had to race with her. Hippomenes distracted Atalanta by throwing three golden apples, one at a time, along the course. He won the race and the bride.

PARTICIPIAL PHRASE: starts with a participle (see p. 79)

Throwing the apple, Hippomenes delayed Atalanta.
|
present active participle of to throw

The apples, **thrown** to the side, were tempting.
|
perfect passive participle of to throw

INFINITIVE PHRASE: starts with an infinitive (see p. 53)

Atalanta was not angry **to lose** the race.
└─┬─┘
infinitive

Hippomenes was willing **to win** dishonestly.
└──┬──┘
infinitive

VERB PHRASE: starts with auxiliary verb or word (see p. 75)

Atalanta **was running** her best in the races.
└────┬────┘
auxiliary verb + main verb

Hippomenes **had watched** others lose.
└─────┬─────┘
auxiliary word + main verb

To recognize the various types of phrases you need to recognize the individual parts (prepositions, participles, infinitives) and then isolate all those words within groups of words which work as a unit of meaning. If this unit of meaning does not have both a subject and a conjugated verb, it is a phrase; if it does have a subject and verb, it is a clause (see below).

WHAT IS A CLAUSE?

A CLAUSE is a group of words containing a subject and a conjugated verb which work as a unit of meaning in a sentence. It can also include a variety of modifiers, such as adjectives and adverbs. There are two kinds of clauses: main and subordinate clauses.

- A MAIN CLAUSE, or INDEPENDENT CLAUSE, generally expresses a complete thought, the important idea of the sentence. If it were taken out of the sentence, it could stand alone as a complete sentence.

- A SUBORDINATE CLAUSE, or DEPENDENT CLAUSE, cannot stand alone as a complete sentence because of the subordinating conjunction. It must always be combined with a main clause.

Either the main or the subordinate clause can come at the beginning of a sentence.

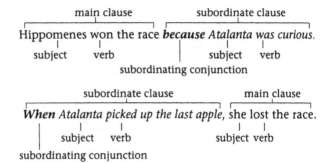

80

90

IN ENGLISH

There is no set position for the verb in an English sentence or clause, but the subject usually comes before the verb.

IN LATIN

In a sentence or main clause, the conjugated verb usually stands last. The subject usually stands near the beginning.

Hippomenēs Atalantam in mātrimōnium **dūxit**.
*Hippomenes married [**led** into matrimony] Atalanta.*

TYPES OF SENTENCES: SIMPLE, COMPOUND, AND COMPLEX

WHAT IS A SIMPLE SENTENCE?

A SIMPLE SENTENCE consists of only one main clause with no

100 subordinate clause.

*Atalanta **loved** the winner.*
Atalanta victōrem **amābat**.
subject   object   verb

In Latin, a variety of word order is possible depending on what is being stressed.

Even before the race Atalanta loved the winner.
Etiam ante certāmen Atalanta victōrem amābat.
The time element, *even before the race*, is being stressed.

110 Victōrem Atalanta etiam ante certāmen amābat.
The winner is being stressed. Atalanta loved him and not someone else.

In a question, the ending -**ne** is usually attached to the first word, and since the verb is such a strong element, it often stands first with the -**ne** ending.

Amābatne Atalanta victōrem etiam ante certāmen?
verb + -**ne**
Did Atalanta love the winner even before the race?

WHAT IS A COMPOUND SENTENCE?

A COMPOUND SENTENCE consists of two main clauses joined by a coordinating conjunction (see *What is a Conjunction?*, p. 99).

120

```
        main clause 1              main clause 2
   ┌──────────────────┐   ┌────────────────────────┐
   Venus helped the lovers, but they were not grateful.
    │     │              │    │      │
   subject verb          │ subject verb
                   coordinating
                   conjunction
```

Venus amantēs **iūvit**, sed hī grātī nōn **erant**.

WHAT IS A COMPLEX SENTENCE?

A COMPLEX SENTENCE consists of a main clause and one or more subordinate clauses (see p. 99).

130

```
           main clause              subordinate clause
   ┌──────────────────────┐   ┌──────────────────────────┐
   Atalanta did not win in the race because she had picked up the apples.
    │     └──┬──┘                        │
   subject  verb              subordinating conjunction
```

Atalanta certāmine nōn **superāvit** quod pōma carpserat.

 REVIEW

I. Circle whether the sentences below are simple (S), compound (C) or complex (Cx).

1. Orpheus married Eurydice, but his bride died.

          S   C   Cx

2. Eurydice went to the Underworld, and Orpheus tried to bring her back.

          S   C   Cx

3. Because Orpheus looked back, Eurydice had to return to the Underworld.

          S   C   Cx

II. Circle whether the following are phrases (P), clauses (C), or sentences (S). (Punctuation and capitalization have purposely been omitted.)

1. afterwards Orpheus denying all love of women and only singing his sad songs   P   C   S

2. because the angry Maenads were throwing rocks at Orpheus   P   C   S

3. at first the rocks fell at the feet of Orpheus, conquered by the songs of the bard   P   C   S

4. finally the shouts of the Maenads and the drums overcame the song of Orpheus   P   C   S

106

CHAPTER

33

WHAT ARE DECLARATIVE, INTERROGATIVE, AFFIRMATIVE, AND NEGATIVE SENTENCES?

Sentences are identified by type:
whether they make statements, ask questions, or
express affirmative or negative ideas.

A **DECLARATIVE SENTENCE** is a sentence that makes a statement.
The Greeks invaded Troy.[1]

An **INTERROGATIVE SENTENCE** is a sentence that asks a question.
Why did the Greeks invade Troy?

An **AFFIRMATIVE** sentence makes a statement without a negative word such as *not, never, nobody, nothing.*
The Greeks *invaded* Troy.

A **NEGATIVE** sentence makes a statement with a negative word such as *not, never, nobody, nothing.*
The Greeks *did not invade* Rome.

IN ENGLISH

A declarative sentence can be changed to an interrogative sentence in several ways:

- by placing the verb *to do (do* or *does* for a question in the present tense, *did* for the past tense), or the word *will* or *shall* for the future tense, before the subject of the sentence and changing the main verb to the dictionary form (see *What is the Present Tense?*, p. 63; *What is the Past Tense?*, p. 65; and *What is the Future Tense?*, p. 71).

DECLARATIVE SENTENCE	INTERROGATIVE SENTENCE
Paris *carries off* Helen.	*Does* Paris *carry off* Helen?
present tense	present of *to do* + dictionary form
The Greeks *invaded* Troy.	*Did* the Greeks *invade* Troy?
simple past tense	past of *to do* + dictionary form
The Greeks *will invade* Troy.	*Will* the Greeks *invade* Troy?
future tense	future + dictionary form

[1]The Trojan War was fought to bring back the beautiful Helen from Troy where she had been taken by Paris, a Trojan prince. The Greeks built the Trojan Horse as a device to enter the city and capture it.

- by inverting the normal word order of subject + verb (V) to verb + subject. This INVERSION process can also be used with auxiliary verbs (AV) or auxiliary words (AW).

DECLARATIVE SENTENCE

The Greeks are now in Troy.
subject + V

The Greeks were invading Troy.
subject + AV + main verb

Helen will appear tomorrow.
subject + AW + main verb

INTERROGATIVE SENTENCE

Are the Greeks now in Troy?
V + subject

Were the Greeks invading Troy?
AV + subject + main verb

Will Helen appear tomorrow?
AW + subject + main verb

40

- by adding a short phrase, sometimes called a TAG, at the end of the statement. A tag is used when you expect a "yes" or "no" answer.

The Greeks didn't invade Rome, *did they?* ["No" answer expected.]
The Greeks are now in Troy, *aren't they?* ["Yes" answer expected.]

50

An affirmative sentence can be changed to a negative sentence in several ways:

- by adding *not* after auxiliary words or auxiliary verbs (see *What is an Auxiliary Verb?*, p. 75)

AFFIRMATIVE	NEGATIVE
Winds *are* blowing.	Winds *are not* blowing.
Ships *could* sail.	Ships *could not* sail.
The Greeks *will* sail.	The Greeks *will not* sail.

Frequently, the word *not* is attached to the verb and the letter "o" is replaced by an apostrophe; this is called a CONTRACTION: *is not → isn't; cannot → can't; will not → won't.*

60

- by placing the verb *to do* + *not* (*do not* or *does not* for a negative in the present tense, *did not* for the past tense) or the word *will* + *not* or *shall* + *not* for the future tense, and changing the main verb to the dictionary form

AFFIRMATIVE	NEGATIVE
Venus *aids* Trojans.	Venus *does not aid* Trojans.
Athena *helped* Greeks.	Athena *did not help* Greeks.
Ulysses *will go* home.	Ulysses *will not go* home.

70

IN LATIN

A declarative sentence can be changed to an interrogative sentence in one of two ways.

1. by adding **-ne** to the first word in the sentence. The answer can be either "yes" or "no."

DECLARATIVE SENTENCE	INTERROGATIVE SENTENCE
Graecī Trōiam invādēbant.	Invādēbantne Trōiam Graecī?
The Greeks were invading Troy.	*Were the Greeks invading Troy?*

The verb often appears first in a question since it is the word being stressed.

2. by using the Latin equivalent of a tag which is placed at the beginning of the sentence. **Nōnne** is used when a "yes" answer is expected and **Num** is used when a "no" answer is expected.

Nōnne Graecī Trōiam invāsērunt? ["Yes" answer expected.]
*The Greeks invaded Troy, **didn't they?***

Num Graecī Rōmam invāsērunt? ["No" answer expected.]
*The Greeks did not invade Rome, **did they?***

An affirmative sentence can be changed to a negative sentence by adding the word **nōn** *(not)* before the verb.:

Graecī Rōmam **nōn** invāsērunt.
*The Greeks **did not** invade Rome.*

✎ REVIEW

I. Change the following statements into questions.
- Make each of the sentences above negative.

1. The Greeks won the war.

_____?

_____

2. Helen loved Paris.

_____?

_____

3. Helen will return home.

_____?

_____

II. Write a tag question expecting a "yes" answer.
- Write a tag question expecting a "no" answer.

Helen loved Paris.

_____

_____

WHAT IS MEANT BY DIRECT AND INDIRECT STATEMENTS?

A DIRECT STATEMENT is the transmission of a message
between a speaker and a listener.
The message is set in quotation marks.

> Caesar says, "I came, I saw, I conquered."
> Cicero said, "My city is in danger."

An INDIRECT STATEMENT is the reporting of the message
without quoting the words directly.

> Caesar says (that) he came, he saw, he conquered.
> Cicero said (that) his city was in danger.

IN ENGLISH

When a direct statement is changed to an indirect statement, the words between quotations have to be adapted
to reported speech.

1. They become a subordinate clause introduced by "that"
(see p. 103). Since "that" is frequently omitted in
English, we have put it between parentheses.
2. If these words contain pronouns or possessive adjectives, they are changed to reflect the change of speaker.
3. The verb tense is shifted in order to maintain the logical
time sequence.

DIRECT STATEMENT   Cicero said, "*My* city *is* in danger."
                                   past   present

INDIRECT STATEMENT   Cicero said (that) *his* city *was* in danger.
                                   past   past

DIRECT STATEMENT   Cicero said, "*My* city *was* in danger."
                                   past   past

INDIRECT STATEMENT   Cicero said (that) *his* city *had been* in danger.
                                   past   past perfect

DIRECT STATEMENT   Cicero said, "*My* city *will be* in danger."
                                   past   future

INDIRECT STATEMENT   Cicero said (that) *his* city *would be* in danger.
                                   past   auxiliary "would" + verb

IN LATIN

The indirect statement construction is commonly used in Latin. It is used not only after verbs of saying, but also after verbs of thinking, feeling, sensing, and the like. It is important to recognize the indirect statement construction following verbs such as the ones listed above since that construction follows special rules: the subject is in the accusative case and the verb is in the infinitive.

*Caesar says **(that)** he came, he saw, he conquered.*
Caesar dīcit sē vēnisse, vīdisse, vīcisse.

         subject   verbs
         acc.   infinitive (perfect)

*Cicero said **(that)** his city was in danger.*
Cicero dīxit suam **urbem esse** in perīculō.

         subject   verb
         acc.   infinitive (present)

N.B. Since the introductory word "that" is often omitted at the beginning of an English subordinate clause, you will have to practice recognizing clauses that will require an indirect statement construction in Latin.

SELECTION OF THE INFINITIVE TENSES

Remember that there are three tenses of infinitives in Latin: present, perfect, and future (see *What is an Infinitive?*, p. 53). The infinitive tense selected for the indirect statement depends on when the action of the reported statement, i.e., the subordinate clause, occurred relative to the action of the verb of the main clause.

PRESENT INFINITIVE — action of subordinate clause at the same time as the action of the main verb.

*Cicero **thinks** (that) his city is in danger.*

         at the same time as "Cicero *thinks*"

Cicerō **putat** urbem suam **esse** in perīculō.

   present indicative   present infinitive

PERFECT INFINITIVE — action of subordinate clause before the action of the main verb.

*Cicero **thinks** (that) his city **was** in danger.*

         before "Cicero *thinks*"

Cicerō **putat** urbem suam **fuisse** in perīculō.

   present indicative   perfect infinitive

FUTURE INFINITIVE — action of subordinate clause after the action of the main verb. [80]

Cicero thinks (that) his city will be in danger.

after "Cicero *thinks*"

Cicerō **putat** urbem suam **futūram esse** in perīculō.

present indicative   future infinitive

If we change the main verb from the present tense, "Cicero *thinks*," to the past tense, "Cicero *thought*," the Latin infinitives would be the same as above but they would have to be translated differently into English to [90] maintain the time relationship between the action of the main verb and the subordinate clause.

Cicerō **putāvit** urbem suam **esse** in perīculō.

perfect indicative   present infinitive

Cicero thought (that) his city was in danger.

at the same time as "Cicero *thought*"

Cicerō **putāvit** urbem suam **fuisse** in perīculō.

perfect indicative   perfect infinitive   [100]

Cicero thought (that) his city had been in danger.

before "Cicero *thought*"

Cicerō **putāvit** urbem suam **futūram esse** in perīculō.

perfect indicative   future infinitive

Cicero thought (that) his city would be in danger.

after "Cicero *thought*"

Consult your textbook for a complete discussion of indirect statements.

 REVIEW

I. Change the direct statements below to indirect statements.

1. Cassandra says,"Troy is falling."

_____

2. Cassandra thought, "Trojan women were slaves."

_____

3. Cassandra told the king, "Your wife will kill us."

_____

II. Change the indirect statements to direct statements.

1. Caesar feels that he is in danger.

Caesar feels, "_____"

2. Caesar's wife thinks that he no longer loves her.

Caesar's wife thinks, " _____"

3. They said that his friends had killed him.

They said, " _____"

III. Underline the subordinate clause in the following indirect statements.

- Circle whether the action of the subordinate clause is at the same time as the main verb (=), before the time of the main verb (-), after the time of the main verb (+).
- Indicate which Latin infinitive tense would be used in the subordinate clause: present infinitive (PI), perfect infinitive (PFI), or future infinitive (FI)

1. Caesar thinks that his friends love him.

$$= \quad - \quad + \qquad PI \quad PFI \quad FI$$

Caesar thought that his friends loved him.

$$= \quad - \quad + \qquad PI \quad PFI \quad FI$$

2. Caesar thinks that his friends loved him.

$$= \quad - \quad + \qquad PI \quad PFI \quad FI$$

Caesar thought that his friends had loved him.

$$= \quad - \quad + \qquad PI \quad PFI \quad FI$$

3. Caesar thinks that his friends will love him.

$$= \quad - \quad + \qquad PI \quad PFI \quad FI$$

Caesar thought that his friends would love him.

$$= \quad - \quad + \qquad PI \quad PFI \quad FI$$

WHAT IS MEANT BY DIRECT AND INDIRECT QUESTIONS?

A DIRECT QUESTION is the transmission of the exact words of   1
a question between a speaker and a listener.
> The question is set in quotation marks.
> Paris asked, "Where is Helen?"
> Helen wondered, "When are the Greeks coming?"

An INDIRECT QUESTION is the reporting of another person's
question without quoting the exact words.
> Paris asked where Helen was.
> Helen wondered when the Greeks were coming.   10

IN ENGLISH

When a direct question is changed to an indirect question
the words between quotations have to be adapted to
reported speech.

1. The words between quotations become a subordinate
   clause introduced by the same interrogative word that
   introduced the direct question.
2. If the subordinate clause contains words such as pronouns or possessive adjectives, they are changed to
   reflect the change of subject.   20
3. The verb tense of the subordinate clause is shifted in
   order to maintain the logical time sequence.

DIRECT QUESTION	Priam *asked*, "Who *are* the Greeks?"
↓	past present
INDIRECT QUESTION	Priam *asked* who the Greeks *were*.
	past past
DIRECT QUESTION	Paris *asked*, "Where *was* Helen?"
↓	past past 30
INDIRECT QUESTION	Paris *asked* where Helen *had been*.
	past past perfect
DIRECT QUESTION	Paris *wondered*, "How *did I fail*?"
↓	past past
INDIRECT QUESTION	Paris *wondered* how he *had failed*.
	past past perfect

IN LATIN

The indirect question construction is commonly used in Latin. The quoted question becomes a subordinate clause introduced by the same interrogative word that introduced the direct question, such as **cūr**, *why*; **quis**, *who*; **quid**, *what*; **quandō**, *when*; **ubi**, *where*; **quōmodo**, *how*, etc. It is important to recognize the indirect question construction since it follows special rules: the verb of the main clause remains in the indicative mood, but the verb of the indirect question changes to the subjunctive mood (see *What is the Subjunctive Mood?*, p. 97).

Paris **rogat** ubi Helena **sit**.
　　　　 |　　　　　　　　 |
　 present　　　　 present
　 indicative　　　 subjunctive

*Paris **asks** where Helen **is**.*

Paris **rogāvit** ubi Helena **esset**.
　　　　 |　　　　　　　　 |
　 perfect　　　　 imperfect
　 indicative　　　 subjunctive

*Paris **asked** where Helen **was**.*

SEQUENCE OF TENSES FOR INDIRECT QUESTIONS

The verb of the subordinate clause can be in one of the four Latin subjunctive tenses: present, perfect, imperfect or pluperfect. The subjunctive tense chosen follows a pattern called **SEQUENCE OF TENSES** which is based on two factors:

1. the tense of the verb of the main clause
2. the time of the action of the verb of the subordinate clause relative to the time of the action of the verb of the main clause: before, at the same time, or after

The sequence of tenses is divided into two groups depending on the tense of the verb of the main clause: **PRIMARY SEQUENCE** or **SECONDARY SEQUENCE**.

Primary sequence — The verb of the main clause is in the present, future, or future perfect tense of the indicative mood.

- The verb of the subordinate clause takes place at the same time or after the action of the verb of the main clause → present subjunctive.

*Paris **asks** where Helen **is**.*
　　　　　　　　　　　 |
　 at the same time "Paris *asks*"

Paris **rogat** ubi Helena **sit**.
　　　　 |　　　　　　　　 |
　 present　　　　 present
　 indicative　　　 subjunctive

*Paris **asks** where Helen **will be**.*

after "Paris *asks*"

Paris **rogat** ubi Helena futura **sit**.

present   future active participle +
indicative   present subjunctive of **esse**

- The verb of the subordinate clause takes place before the action of the verb of the main clause → perfect subjunctive

*Paris **asks** where Helen **was**.*

before "Paris *asks*"

Paris **rogat** ubi Helena **fuerit**.

present   perfect
indicative   subjunctive

Secondary sequence — The verb of the main clause is in the imperfect, perfect, or pluperfect tense of the indicative mood.

- The verb of the subordinate clause takes place at the same time or after the action of the verb of the main clause → imperfect subjunctive.

*Paris **asked** where Helen **was**.*

at the same time "Paris *asked*"

Paris **rogāvit** ubi Helena **esset**.

perfect   imperfect
indicative   subjunctive

*Paris **asked** where Helen **would be**.*

after "Paris *asked*"

Paris **rogāvit** ubi Helena futura **esset**.

perfect   future active participle +
indicative   imperfect subjunctive of **esse**

- The verb of the subordinate clause takes place before the action of the verb of the main clause → pluperfect subjunctive.

*Paris **asked** where Helen **had been**.*

before "Paris *asked*"

Paris **rogāvit** ubi Helena **fuisset**.

perfect   pluperfect
indicative   subjunctive

Below is a chart of **Sequence of Tenses** you can use as reference. It is used in many subjunctive constructions.

130

MAIN CLAUSE ↓	SUBORDINATE CLAUSE ↓
Indicative	**Subjunctive**
	Primary sequence
present, future, or future perfect	present (same time as main verb) future active participle + present of **esse** (after the main verb) perfect (time prior to main verb)
	Secondary sequence
imperfect, perfect, or pluperfect	imperfect (same time as main verb) future active participle + imperfect of **esse** (after the main verb) pluperfect (time prior to main verb)

 REVIEW

I. Change the direct questions below to indirect questions.

1. Clytemnestra asked, "Why is my daughter being taken?"

_____

2. Agamemnon asked, "Why is my daughter being sacrificed?"

_____

3. Iphigenia wondered, "Why are the priests standing there?"

_____

II. Circle whether the verb sequence in the following sentences is primary (PRIM) or secondary (SEC).

1. The Trojans wondered what the strange animal was.

PRIM   SEC

2. Helen asked who was leading the Greeks.

PRIM   SEC

3. Priam asks where his son Hector is.

PRIM   SEC

4. The Greeks wonder when they can attack.

PRIM   SEC

5. Helen will ask when Menelaus is coming to claim her.

PRIM   SEC

CHAPTER

WHAT ARE CONDITIONAL SENTENCES?

CONDITIONAL SENTENCES are those which state that
if a certain condition exists, then
a certain result can be expected.

$$\overbrace{\text{condition}}^{} \qquad \overbrace{\text{result}}^{}$$

If Theseus finds the Minotaur, he will kill him.

IN ENGLISH

Conditional sentences are complex sentences (see
p. 105) consisting of two parts:

- A CONDITION — The subordinate clause introduced by *if*
  or *unless*.
- A RESULT — The main clause which is the result of the
  condition.

condition   result
subordinate clause main clause

If you touch the flame, you will be burned.

There are three types of conditional sentences.

1. SIMPLE CONDITIONS — The condition can take place in the
   present, past, or future.

   PRESENT   If you *say* this, you *are mistaken.*
                present   present

   PAST   If you *said* this, you *were mistaken.*
                past   past

   FUTURE   If you *say* this, you *will be mistaken.*
                present   future

   Although the verb "say" is in the present tense, a future
   time is implied (see p. 71).

2. "SHOULD-WOULD" CONDITIONS — Some doubt is implied
   about the possibility of the condition occurring.

   If you *should say* this, you *would be mistaken.*

3. CONTRARY-TO-FACT CONDITIONS — There is no possibility of
   the condition actually occurring. These statements can
   only be made about the present or past.

PRESENT   If my friend *were* here, I would be happy.
                |
             subjunctive
IMPLICATION: My friend is not here. (*Were* is an example of
one of the rare uses of the subjunctive, see p. 97.)

PAST   If my friend *had been* here, I would have been happy.
                 └─┬─┘
               past perfect indicative
IMPLICATION: My friend was not here.

IN LATIN

The same three types of conditional sentences exist with almost the same sequence of tenses.

1. SIMPLE CONDITIONS — The various tenses of the indicative mood are used in both clauses.

Sī hoc **dīcis, errās.**
     | |
   present   present
   indicative indicative
*If you **say** this, you **are mistaken.***
    | └──┬──┘
  present   present

Sī hoc **dīxistī, errāvistī.**
     | |
   perfect   perfect
   indicative indicative

*If you **said** this, you **were mistaken.***
   | └───┬───┘
   past   past

Sī hoc **dīcēs, errābis.**
    | |
  future   future
  indicative indicative
*If you **say** (**will say**) this, you **will be mistaken.***

    | └──┬──┘
  present   future
  action 1   action 2

Sī hoc **dīxeris, errābis.**

      | |
 future perfect future
 indicative   indicative
*If you **say** (**will have said**) this, you **will be mistaken.***
   | └───┬───┘
  present   future
  action 1   action 2

In the last two examples, although the English present tense is used for action 1, a future time is implied. Since action 1 will take place before action 2 in the future, in Latin action 1 is in the future perfect tense and action 2 is in the future tense (see *What is the Future Tense?*, p. 71 and *What is the Future Perfect Tense?*, p. 73).

2. "SHOULD-WOULD" CONDITIONS — The present subjunctive is used in both clauses. As in English, there is some doubt about the condition occurring. Since the word "should" is often omitted by English speakers, we have placed it between parentheses. 80

> Sī hoc dīcās, errēs.
> | |
> present   present
> subjunctive subjunctive
> *If you (should) say this, you **would be mistaken**.*

3. CONTRARY-TO-FACT CONDITIONS —Either the imperfect subjunctive or the pluperfect subjunctive is used in both clauses. As in English, there is no possibility of the condition occurring. 90

> PRESENT   Sī amīcus meus nunc **adesset**, laetus **essem**.
> | |
>   imperfect   imperfect
>   subjunctive subjunctive
> *If my friend **were** here, I **would be** happy.*

> PAST   Sī amīcus meus herī **adfuisset**, laetus **fuissem**.
> | |
>   pluperfect   pluperfect 100
>   subjunctive subjunctive
> *If my friend **had been** here, I **would have been** happy.*

 REVIEW

Circle whether the conditional sentences below are simple (S), "should-would" (SW), or contrary-to-fact (CF).

1. If the sailors go to the palace, Circe will turn them into pigs.

    S   SW   CF

2. If Ulysses should go to the palace, Circe would be overjoyed.

    S   SW   CF

3. If Circe were kind, she would not change men into pigs.

    S   SW   CF

4. If Ulysses were home, he would not have to worry about Circe.

    S   SW   CF

5. If Mercury should appear, he would save Ulysses and his men.

    S   SW   CF

WHAT IS AN ADJECTIVE?

An **ADJECTIVE** is a word that describes a noun or a pronoun.
There are different types of adjectives
which are classified according to the way
they describe or modify a noun or pronoun.

DESCRIPTIVE ADJECTIVE — A descriptive adjective indicates a quality of a noun or pronoun (see p. 121).

> Helen was a *beautiful* woman.
> Her husband was Menelaus. He was very *jealous.*

POSSESSIVE ADJECTIVE— A possessive adjective shows possession indicating who owns the noun (see p. 131).

> Helen betrayed *her* husband.
> The Greeks sacked Troy to bring back *their* queen.

INTERROGATIVE ADJECTIVE — An interrogative adjective asks a question about a noun (see p. 135).

> *Whose* queen was abducted?
> *What* war was fought to bring her back?

DEMONSTRATIVE ADJECTIVE — A demonstrative adjective points out a noun (see p. 138).

> *This* hero was brave.
> *That* prince was a coward.

IN ENGLISH

English adjectives usually do not change their form, regardless of the noun or pronoun described.

IN LATIN

Latin adjectives describe nouns and pronouns in the same way as do English adjectives. The principal difference is that in Latin an adjective always agrees in case, gender, and number with the noun or pronoun it describes.

WHAT IS A DESCRIPTIVE ADJECTIVE?

A **DESCRIPTIVE ADJECTIVE** is a word that indicates a quality of a
noun or pronoun. As the name indicates, it
describes that noun or pronoun.

> A *beautiful* woman was the cause of the *tragic* Trojan War.
> descriptive noun   descriptive   noun
> adjective   described   adjective   described

IN ENGLISH

A descriptive adjective does not change form, regardless of
the noun or pronoun it modifies.

> He has *bright* eyes.
> There is a *bright* star in the sky.

>> The form of the adjective *bright* remains the same although
>> the nouns described are different in number *(eyes* is plural
>> and *star* is singular).

Descriptive adjectives are divided into two groups
depending on how they are connected to the noun they
modify.

1. An **ATTRIBUTIVE ADJECTIVE** usually precedes the noun it
   modifies.

   > She lived in a *large* house.
   > attributive noun
   > adjective   described

   > We are looking at a *bright* star.
   > attributive noun
   > adjective   described

2. A **PREDICATE ADJECTIVE** follows a **LINKING VERB**: *to be, to feel,*
   to look, etc. (see p. 32) and refers back to the subject.

   > The house appears *large.*
   > noun   linking predicate
   > described   verb   adjective

   > The teacher seems *kind.*
   > noun   linking predicate
   > described   verb   adjective

1

10

20

30

IN LATIN

As in English, descriptive adjectives can be identified as attributive or predicate according to the way they are connected to the noun they describe. Unlike in English where attributive adjectives precede the noun modified, in Latin the placement of attributive adjectives depends on the type of adjective: adjectives of description usually follow the noun modified, but adjectives of size or quantity generally precede.

While English descriptive adjectives never change form, all Latin descriptive adjectives, attributive and predicate, change form in order to agree in case, gender, and number with the noun or pronoun they modify.

Oculōs **clārōs** habet.

acc. masc. pl.

He has bright eyes.

Magnum templum spectāmus.

acc. neut. sing.

We are looking at the large temple.

IDENTIFYING AN ADJECTIVE'S DECLENSION

Adjectives follow the same declension patterns as nouns. We have divided the declension of adjectives into two groups, called Group A and Group B.

1. **GROUP A** — Adjectives of the 1ˢᵗ and 2ⁿᵈ declension merged into a single group. These adjectives are called "1ˢᵗ and 2ⁿᵈ declension" because the masculine and neuter forms have endings that are declined like nouns of the 2ⁿᵈ declension and the feminine forms have endings that are declined like nouns of the 1ˢᵗ declension. Most of the adjectives in this group are identifiable by their three-form dictionary entry ending in **-us, -a, -um**.

dictionary entry   bonus, -a, -um   *good*
fully written   bonus, bona, bonum

masc.   fem.   neut.

	SINGULAR			PLURAL		
	2ⁿᵈ decl. Masc.	1ˢᵗ decl. Fem.	2ⁿᵈ decl. Neut.	2ⁿᵈ decl. Masc.	1ˢᵗ decl. Fem.	2ⁿᵈ decl Neut.
Nom.	bonus	bona	bonum	bonī	bonae	bona
Gen.	bonī	bonae	bonī	bonōrum	bonārum	bonōrum
Dat.	bonō	bonae	bonō	bonīs	bonīs	bonīs
Acc.	bonum	bonam	bonum	bonōs	bonās	bona
Abl.	bonō	bonā	bonō	bonīs	bonīs	bonīs

There are several adjectives following this pattern whose nominative masculine singular ends in -**er**. Whether these adjectives keep or drop the -**e**- in the stem is apparent in the feminine and neuter forms given in the vocabulary entry. The rest of the declension is regular.

DICTIONARY ENTRY	miser, -a, -um	pulcher, -chra, -chrum
STEM	miser-	pulchr-
	keeps the "e"	drops the "e"

2. **GROUP B** — Adjectives of the 3ʳᵈ declension follow the declension pattern of nouns of the 3ʳᵈ declension. This group includes all the adjectives which do not belong to Group A. The dictionary entry will show you whether the adjective has one form for all genders, or two or three forms. Consult your textbook for the complete declensions of these adjectives.

TWO FORMS — Most of the adjectives of Group B have two forms: the first for the masculine and feminine genders, and the second for the neuter.

DICTIONARY ENTRY	fidēlis, -e	*faithful*
FULLY WRITTEN	fidēlis, fidēle	
	masc. neut.	
	fem.	

ONE FORM — Some adjectives of Group B have one form for all three genders. Since the stem of the adjective is not always seen in the nominative form, the dictionary entry also includes the complete genitive form.

DICTIONARY ENTRY   audax, **audā**cis *bold*
                    masc.   gen. → **audāc**- stem
                    fem.
                    neut.

THREE FORMS — Some adjectives of Group B have three forms, one for each gender. They can be distinguished from Group A because they do not have that group's -**us**, -**a**, -**um** endings for masculine, feminine and neuter.

DICTIONARY ENTRY   ācer, **ācr**is, **ācr**e *sharp*
                    masc.   fem.   neut. → **ācr**- stem

An adjective can belong to a different declension from the noun it modifies, and thus may have a different ending.

For example, if both the adjective and the noun it modifies belong to the 1ˢᵗ declension they will have the same endings (**in magnīs casīs**, *in large houses*). However, if they belong to different declensions, i.e., an adjective of the 1ˢᵗ declension modifying a noun of the 3ʳᵈ declension, they will have different endings (**in magnīs urbibus**, *in large cities*).

SUMMARY

Here is a chart you can use to determine the declension to which an adjective belongs on the basis of the number of forms listed in the nominative singular.

Group	Nº forms	Decl.	NOMINATIVE SINGULAR Masculine	Feminine	Neuter
A	3	1ˢᵗ		bona	
				misera	
		2ⁿᵈ	bonus		bonum
			miser		miserum
B	3	3ʳᵈ	ācer	ācris	ācre
	2		fidēlis	fidēlis	fidēle
	1		audax	audax	audax

For the proper adjective ending, follow these steps.

1. NOUN MODIFIED — Determine the noun's case, gender, and number.

2. DECLENSION OF ADJECTIVE — Establish the declension of the adjective.

3. SELECTION OF FORM OF ADJECTIVE — Select the proper form of the adjective based on the modified noun's case, gender, and number and on the adjective's declension.

Here are a few examples .

> *Cicero was a **true** orator.*
> 1. NOUN MODIFIED: *orator* → **ōrātor**
>   CASE: nominative (predicate nominative)
>   GENDER & NUMBER: masculine singular
> 2. ADJECTIVE: *true* → **vērus, -a, -um**
>   DECLENSION: masculine Group A 2ⁿᵈ declension
> 3. SELECTION: **orātōr** and **vērus** → nom. masc. sing.
>
> Cicerō erat ōrātor **vērus**.
> | |
>   nom. masc. sing.

> *Many men loved **beautiful** Atalanta.*
> 1. NOUN MODIFIED: *Atalanta* → **Atalanta**
>   CASE: accusative
>   GENDER & NUMBER: feminine singular
> 2. ADJECTIVE: *beautiful* → **pulcher, pulchra, pulchrum**
>   DECLENSION: feminine Group A 1ˢᵗ declension
> 3. SELECTION: **Atalantam** and **pulchram** → acc. fem. sing.
>
> Multī vīrī Atalantam **pulchram** amābant.
> | |
>   acc. fem. sing.

*Medusa was killed with a **sharp** sword.*
1. NOUN MODIFIED: *sword* → **gladiō**
   CASE: ablative
   GENDER & NUMBER: masculine singular
2. ADJECTIVE: *sharp* → **ācer, ācris, ācre**
   DECLENSION: masculine Group B 3ʳᵈ declension
3. SELECTION: **gladiō** and **ācrī** → abl. masc. sing.

Medūsa gladiō **ācrī** necāta est.
       | |
      abl. masc. sing.

*Ulysses loved his **faithful** queen.*
1. NOUN MODIFIED: *queen* → **rēgīnam**
   CASE: accusative
   GENDER & NUMBER: feminine singular
2. ADJECTIVE: *faithful* → **fidēlis, -e**
   DECLENSION: feminine Group B 3ʳᵈ declension
3. SELECTION: **rēgīnam** and **fidēlem** → acc. fem. sing.

Ulixēs rēgīnam **fidēlem** amābat.
     | |
   acc. fem. sing.

*The **bold** Amazons terrified the men.*
1. NOUN MODIFIED: *Amazons* → **Amāzonēs**
   CASE: nominative
   GENDER & NUMBER: feminine plural
2. ADJECTIVE: *bold* → **audax, audācis** (genitive)
   DECLENSION: feminine Group B 3ʳᵈ declension
3. SELECTION: **Amāzonēs** and **audācēs** → nom. fem. pl.

Amāzonēs **audācēs** virōs terruērunt.
    | |
   nom. fem. pl.

170

180

✎ REVIEW

I. In the following sentences circle the gender of the adjective in Latin: masculine (M), feminine (F), or neuter (N).
- Circle the number of the adjective in Latin: singular (S) or plural (P).
- Circle the case of the adjective in Latin: nominative (NOM), genitive (GEN), dative (DAT), accusative (ACC), ablative (ABL).

1. The heroic image of Hercules is a strong man.

image, **imāgō** → feminine; *man*, **vir** → masculine

| heroic | M | F | N | S | P | NOM | GEN | DAT | ACC | ABL |
| strong | M | F | N | S | P | NOM | GEN | DAT | ACC | ABL |

2. Mad Hercules killed his faithful wife.

Hercules, **Hercules** → masculine; *wife*, **uxor** → feminine

| mad | M | F | N | S | P | NOM | GEN | DAT | ACC | ABL |
| faithful | M | F | N | S | P | NOM | GEN | DAT | ACC | ABL |

3. Because he did an evil deed, Hercules had to perform hard labors.

deed, **factum** → neuter; *labor*, **labor** → masculine

evil	M	F	N	S	P		NOM	GEN	DAT	ACC	ABL

harsh	M	F	N	S	P		NOM	GEN	DAT	ACC	ABL

II. For each dictionary entry, circle whether the adjective belongs to Group A (A) or Group B (B).

- For adjectives belonging to Group B indicate if it is of 1, 2, or 3 endings.

1. multus, -a, -um *(many)*

    A   B   1   2   3

2. brevis, -e *(short)*

    A   B   1   2   3

3. longus, -a, -um *(long)*

    A   B   1   2   3

4. crūdēlis, -e *(cruel)*

    A   B   1   2   3

5. ferox, -ōcis *(wild, warlike)*

    A   B   1   2   3

6. celer -eris, -ere *(fast)*

    A   B   1   2   3

7. omnis, -e *(every, all)*

    A   B   1   2   3

WHAT IS MEANT BY COMPARISON OF ADJECTIVES?

The term COMPARISON OF ADJECTIVES is used to refer to the forms of descriptive adjectives used to compare the different qualities of the nouns they modify.

comparison of adjectives

The moon is *bright,* but the sun is *brighter.*

descriptive adjective   comparative degree adjective
modifying *moon*   modifying *sun*

IN ENGLISH

There are three different degrees of comparison.

1. POSITIVE DEGREE — This form refers to the quality of one person or thing. It is simply the basic adjective form (see *What is a Descriptive Adjective?*, p. 121).

> The philosopher is *wise.*
> The moon is *bright.*
> The sword is *expensive.*
> His speech is *interesting.*

2. COMPARATIVE DEGREE — This form compares the quality of one person or thing with that of another person or thing. It is formed differently depending on the length of the adjective.

- by adding *-er* to short adjectives

> The philosopher is *wiser* than many men.
> The sun is *brighter* than the moon.

- by adding the word *more* in front of longer adjectives

> This sword is *more expensive.*
> This orator's speech is *more interesting.*

3. SUPERLATIVE DEGREE — This form is used to stress the highest degree of a quality. It is formed differently depending on the length of the adjective.

- by adding *-est* to short adjectives

> The philosopher is the *wisest* in Athens.
> The sun is the *brightest* star in our heavens.

- by adding the word *most, very,* or *exceedingly* in front of longer adjectives

> This sword is the *most expensive* in Rome.
> Cicero's speech is *very interesting.*

IN LATIN

As in English, descriptive adjectives have three degrees of comparison: positive, comparative, and superlative.

Like all Latin adjectives, comparatives change form in order to agree in case, gender, and number with the noun or pronoun they modify.

1. POSITIVE DEGREE — This form is simply the basic adjective form, i.e., the dictionary form.

> Gladius est **ācer.**
> | |
> noun   adjective positive degree
> └ nom. masc. sing.┘
> *The sword is **sharp.***

2. COMPARATIVE DEGREE — This form is based on the genitive masculine singular stem of the adjective in the positive degree. The comparative degree is formed differently depending on whether the genitive stem ends with a consonant or a vowel.

- Adjectives with a genitive masculine singular positive stem ending with a consonant use that form as a stem + **-ior** (for the masculine and feminine) or **-ius** (for the neuter).

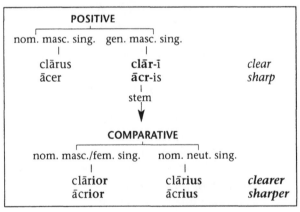

These comparative forms are declined like the two-form adjectives in Group B (see p. 123).

> Hic discipulus respōnsum **clārius** dedit.
> | |
>   noun   adjective comparative degree
>   └ acc. neut. sing.┘
> *This student gave a **clearer** answer.*

Lingua est **ācrior** quam gladius.

noun   adjective comparative degree
    └nom. fem. sing. ┘   80

The tongue is sharper than the sword.

- Adjectives whose genitive masculine singular positive stem ends with a vowel add place the word **magis** (*more,* an adverb that doesn't change form)) before their positive form in the appropriate case .

Vīctōria **magis dubia** nunc vidētur.

noun   adjective comparative degree
  └ nom. fem. sing. ┘

Victory now seems more doubtful.   90

3. SUPERLATIVE DEGREE — The superlative degree is formed differently depending on the ending of the positive adjective. Regardless of the form, all the adjectives of the superlative degree are declined like Group A (see pp. 122-123).

- Most superlatives use the genitive singular stem of the positive form + **-issimus, -a, -um.**

Respōnsum philosophī **clārissimum** erat.

noun   adjective superlative degree
           clār- (gen. sing. stem) + **-issimum**
  └ nom. neut. sing.┘   100

The philosopher's answer was most clear.

- Adjectives with a nominative masculine singular positive form ending in **-er** use that form as a stem + **-rimus, -a, -um.**

Sōcratēs mentem **ācerrimam** habēbat.

noun   adjective superlative degree
        ācer- + **-rimam**
  └ acc. fem. sing. ┘

Socrates had a very sharp mind.   110

- Adjectives with a nominative masculine singular positive form ending with a vowel add the word **maximē** (*most, very,* an adverb that doesn't change form) before their positive form in the appropriate case.

Vīctōria **maximē dubia** nunc vidētur .

noun   adjective superlative degree
  └ nom. fem. sing. ┘

Victory now seems most doubtful.   120

N. B. — In English and in Latin there are frequently used comparative adjectives that are irregular and must be memorized. Because many words used in English are derived from these Latin forms, memorizing them should not be difficult.

Positive (masc.)	Comparative (masc.)	English derivative	Superlative (masc.)	English derivative
bonus *good*	melior *better*	*ameliorate*	optimus *best*	*optimist*
malus *bad*	pēior *worse*	*pejorative*	pessimus *worst*	*pessimist*
magnus *great*	maior *greater*	*major*	maximus *greatest*	*maximum*

SUMMARY

Below is a reference chart summarizing the formation of the comparative and superlative degrees of adjectives .

Positive degree	Comparative degree	Superlative degree
	STEM: genitive singular of positive degree + -**ior** for masc. & fem. + -**ius** for neuter ↓	STEM: genitive singular of positive degree + -**issimus, -a, -um** OR STEM: nominative singular of positive degree + -**rimus, -a, -um** ↓
↓	GROUP B: 3rd declension	GROUP A: 1st/2nd declension
clārus, -a, -um clār- → gen. stem	clārior, clārius	clārissimus, -a, -um
ācer, ācris, ācre ācr- → gen. stem	ācrior, ācrius	ācerrimus, -a, -um

 REVIEW

In the sentences below, draw an arrow from the adjective to the noun it modifies.

- Circle the degree of comparison: positive (P), comparative (C), or superlative (S).

1. Blood is thicker than water.   P   C   S

2. Your parents are your best friends.   P   C   S

3. The poet is famous.   P   C   S

4. Poets are more famous than soldiers.   P   C   S

5. Ovid is a most famous poet.   P   C   S

WHAT IS A POSSESSIVE ADJECTIVE?

A POSSESSIVE ADJECTIVE is a word that describes a noun   1
by showing who possesses that noun.

> Whose house is that? It's *his* house.
> *His* shows who possesses the noun *house*.
> The possessor is "he." The thing possessed is *house*.

IN ENGLISH

Like subject pronouns, possessive adjectives are identified
according to the person they represent (see p. 41).

SINGULAR POSSESSOR

1ST PERSON		my	10
2ND PERSON		your
3RD PERSON	MASCULINE	his
	FEMININE	her
	NEUTER	its

PLURAL POSSESSOR

1ST PERSON	our
2ND PERSON	your
3RD PERSON	their

The possessive adjective refers only to the person who   20
possesses, i.e., the possessor.

Aeneas was Venus's son. Venus loved *her* son.
possessor

Aeneas's mother was a goddess. He loved *his* mother.
possessor

Troy's walls were high. Troy did not defend *its* walls.
possessor   30

When the 3rd person singular *(his, her, its)* and plural *(their)*
are used, two meanings are often possible. For example,
the sentence "Medea murdered *her* children" could mean
that Medea murdered her own children or someone else's
children. Usually the context of the sentence helps us
understand the correct meaning. However, when there is

a possibility of a misunderstanding, the word "own" is added after the possessive adjective: "Medea murdered *her own* children." In this case, and whenever *own* can be added after the possessive adjective, the possessive adjective is called REFLEXIVE; it "reflects back" to the possessor which is usually the subject of the sentence or clause.

The goddess saw *her* father. [*her own* father]

If the possessive adjective refers to a possessor other than the subject of the sentence or clause, it is called NON-REFLEXIVE.

The goddess saw *her* (the nymph's) father. [*someone else's* father]

IN LATIN

As in English, a Latin possessive adjective changes to identify the possessor, but like most Latin adjectives it must agree in case, number, and gender with the noun possessed.

All the Latin possessive adjectives are declined according to Group A (see pp. 122-3). The 3rd person possessive adjective **suus, -a, -um** is reflexive, and can only have the "own" meaning, *his own, her own, its own,* and *their own.*

Here are the steps you should follow to choose the correct possessive adjective and its proper form:

1. POSSESSOR: Indicate the possessor with the stem of the possessive adjective.

   SINGULAR
my	me-
your	tu-
his, her, its (own)	su-

   PLURAL
our	nostr- [nom. sing. **noster**]
your	vestr- [nom. sing. **vester**]
their (own)	su-

2. NOUN POSSESSED: Identify the case, gender, and number of the noun possessed.

3. SELECTION: Provide the ending of the possessive adjective which reflects the case, gender, and number of the noun possessed.

   Citizens, the walls of your city are not high enough!
   1. POSSESSOR: *your* (many people) → 2nd per. pl. → **vestr-**
   2. NOUN POSSESSED: *city* → **urbs**
      CASE: possessive → genitive
      GENDER & NUMBER: feminine singular
   3. SELECTION: **vestrae** → genitive feminine singular
   Cīvēs, moenia urbis **vestrae** nōn sunt satis alta.

*Aeneas loved **his** mother.*   80
   1. POSSESSOR: *his* → 3rd per. sing. reflexive → **su-**
   2. NOUN POSSESSED: *mother* → **māter**
      CASE: direct object → accusative
      GENDER & NUMBER: feminine singular
   3. SELECTION: **suam** → accusative feminine singular
Aenēas mātrem **suam** amābat.

*Venus often gave comfort to **her** son.*
   1. POSSESSOR: *her* → 3rd per. sing. reflexive → **su-**
   2. NOUN POSSESSED: *son* → **fīlius**
      CASE: indirect object → dative
      GENDER & NUMBER: masculine singular
   3. SELECTION: **suō** → dative masculine singular   90
Venus fīliō **suō** consōlātiōnem saepe dedit.

For the 3rd person non-reflexive possessive adjectives, Latin uses the genitive case of the personal pronoun (see p. 45), regardless of the case of the noun modified. These forms: singular → **eius**; plural → **eōrum** (masc. & neut. pl.) and **eārum** (fem. pl.), have endings reflecting the gender and number of the possessor. The literal meaning is *of him, of her, of it, of them*, i.e. **librī eōrum** → *the books of them (their books).*

*The goddess saw **her** father.* [referring to the goddess' father]   100
Dea patrem **eius** vīdit.

    3rd person personal pronoun genitive
    fem. sing. (referring to *the goddess)*

Compare to:

*The goddess saw **her** father.* [referring to her own father]
Dea patrem **suum** vīdit.

    3rd person reflexive possessive adjective
    acc. masc. sing. agrees with case, gender, and number of
    patrem *(father)*

N.B. Possessive adjectives are frequently omitted in Latin if   110
there is no doubt as to who is the possessor. However, you should add them in the English translation.

Eurōpa cum amīcīs lūdit.
*Europa is playing with **her** friends.*

REVIEW

Underline the possessive adjectives in the following English sentences.

■ Fill in the requested information.
■ Indicate the gender and number of the possessive adjective in Latin: masculine (M), feminine (F), or neuter (N); singular (S) or plural (P).
■ Complete the Latin possessive adjective.

1. We love our mothers.

    NOUN POSSESSED: _____
    ■ FUNCTION: _____ → CASE: _____
    ■ GENDER & NUMBER: M   F   N   S   P
    SELECTION: _____
    Mātrēs nostr_____ amāmus.

2. You love your mothers.

    NOUN POSSESSED: _____
    ■ FUNCTION: _____ → CASE: _____
    ■ GENDER & NUMBER: M   F   N   S   P
    SELECTION: _____
    Mātrēs vestr_____ amātis.

3. They love their (own) mothers.

    REFLEXIVE/NON-REFLEXIVE: R   NON-R
    NOUN POSSESSED: _____
    ■ FUNCTION: _____ → CASE: _____
    ■ GENDER & NUMBER: M   F   N   S   P
    SELECTION: _____
    Mātrēs su_____ amant.

4. The girls love their (boyfriends') mothers.

    REFLEXIVE/NON-REFLEXIVE: R   NON-R
    ■ CASE PERSONAL PRONOUN: _____
    POSSESSOR: _____
    ■ GENDER & NUMBER: M   F   N   S   P
    SELECTION: _____
    Mātrēs e_____ amant.

WHAT IS AN INTERROGATIVE ADJECTIVE?

An **INTERROGATIVE ADJECTIVE** is a word that asks for information about a noun.

> *Which* book do you want?
> asks information about the noun *book*

IN ENGLISH

The words *which, what* and *whose* are called interrogative adjectives when they come in front of a noun and are used to ask a question about that noun.

> *Which* instructor is teaching the course?
> noun
>
> *What* courses are you taking?
> *Whose* book is on the table?[1]

IN LATIN

There are four types of interrogative adjectives, and the one used depends on the type of information being asked about the noun. As all Latin adjectives, interrogative adjectives must agree with the noun they modify in case, number, and gender (follow the steps on p. 124).

1. **what** *[is the name of, what kind of — referring to an inherent characteristic of its antecedent]* → **quī, quae, quod** declined in all cases like the relative pronoun **quī, quae, quod** (see p. 158). Consult your textbook for the complete declension.

> **What** *[is the name of the] goddess did Niobe offend? Latona.*
> **Quam** deam Niobē offendit? Lātōnam.
> interr. noun
> adj.
> acc. fem. sing.

> **What** *woman offended the goddess? A proud woman.*
> **Quae** mulier deam offendit? Mulier superba.
> interr. noun
> adj.
> nom. fem. sing.

---

[1]*Whose* can be either an adjective or a pronoun in English, but in Latin it is considered only a pronoun and will be discussed under interrogative pronouns, pp. 147-8.

2. *what [kind of — referring to a variety or degree of its antecedent]* → **quālis, quāle** declined as adjectives of Group B (see p. 123) with two endings.

*With **what** [kind of] punishment did the goddess afflict her?*
With a severe punishment.
Quālī poenā dea eam affēcit? Poenā sevērā.
interr.   noun
adj.
abl. fem. sing.

3. *how much [to what degree]* → **quantus, -a, -um** declined as adjectives of Group A (see pp. 122-3).

*With **what** [how much] sorrow did the mother bewail the dead children? With the greatest sorrow.*
Quantō dolōre māter puerōs mortuōs flēbat? Maximō dolōre.
interr.   noun
adj.
abl. fem. sing.

4. *how many* → **quot** not declined.

*How **many** arrows did Apollo shoot? Seven arrows.*
Quot sagittās Apollo coniēcit? Septem sagittās.
interr.   noun
adj.   acc. fem. pl.

N.B. The word *what* is not always an interrogative adjective. It can also be an interrogative pronoun (see *What is an Interrogative Pronoun?*, p. 143). Remember that the adjective modifies a noun while the pronoun replaces the noun.

What noise is that?

interrogative adjective

What is that?

interrogative pronoun

It is important that you distinguish one from the other, because in Latin different words are used and they follow different rules.

✎ **REVIEW**

Circle the interrogative adjectives in the sentences below.
- Draw an arrow from the interrogative adjective to the noun it modifies.
- Circle the interrogative adjective that would be used in Latin: **quī, quae, quod** (A), **quālis,-e** (B), **quantus, -a, -um** (C), **quot** (D).

1. What man carried off Helen? Paris.   A   B   C   D

2. What kind of man did such an evil deed?   A   B   C   D

3. What kind of crime did he commit?   A   B   C   D

4. How much booty did Paris also steal?   A   B   C   D

5. How many years did the Greeks wage war? A   B   C   D

6. How many Trojans did the Greeks kill?   A   B   C   D

CHAPTER

42

WHAT IS A DEMONSTRATIVE ADJECTIVE?

1 A DEMONSTRATIVE ADJECTIVE is a word used
to point out a noun. The word *demonstrative* comes
from the Latin **dēmōnstrāre** meaning *to point out* or *show.*

This book is interesting.
|
points out the noun *book*

IN ENGLISH

The demonstrative adjectives are *this* and *that* in the singular and *these* and *those* in the plural. They are rare
examples of English adjectives agreeing in number with
the noun they modify: *this* changes to *these* and *that*
changes to *those* when they modify a plural noun.

SINGULAR	PLURAL
this arrow	*these* arrows
that man	*those* men

This and *these* refer to persons or objects near the speaker,
and *that* and *those* refer to persons or objects away from
the speaker.

Cupid has two arrows. *This* arrow is sharp; *that* arrow is dull.[1]
| |
close to speaker   away from speaker

"*These* arrows are my weapons. I do not use *those* weapons."
| |
referring to   referring to
arrows at hand   rocks at a distance

IN LATIN

There are several types of demonstrative adjectives, and the
one used depends on the relationship of the speaker to the
person or thing pointed out. Like all Latin adjectives,
demonstrative adjectives must agree with the noun they
modify in case, number, and gender (follows the steps on
p. 124). Consult your textbook for the complete declensions and for other uses of demonstrative adjectives.

---

[1]Cupid shot Apollo with his sharp arrow, causing the god to fall in love. The
dull arrow shot into Daphne caused her to flee. As Apollo overtook the maid-
en, she was changed into a laurel, which he made his sacred tree.

1. to point out a noun near the writer or speaker in space
   or time (*this, these*) → a form of **hic, haec, hoc**

   This plan [just given] is the best.
   Hoc consilium est optimum.
   dem. noun
   adj.

   nom. neut. sing.   40

   Read these books [which I have here].
   Lege hōs librōs.
   dem. noun
   adj.

   acc. masc. pl.

2. to point out a noun away from the writer or speaker in
   space or time (*that, those*) → a form of **ille, illa, illud**

   That senator [over there] is saying nothing!
   Ille senātor nihil dīcit.   50
   dem. noun
   adj.

   nom. masc. sing.

   We shall always regard the fame of those women.
   Glōriam illārum fēminārum semper observābimus.
   dem.   noun
   adj.

   gen. fem. pl.

3. to point out a noun belonging to the person spoken to,
   frequently implying contempt (*that, those*) → a form of   60
   iste, ista, istud

   That story [of yours] is not pleasing to me.
   Ista fābula est mihi nōn grāta.
   dem. noun
   adj.

   nom. fem. sing.

   That horse [of yours] is not worth anything.
   Iste equus nōn valet.
   dem. noun   70
   adj.

   nom. masc. sing.

Consult your textbook for other uses of Latin demonstrative
adjectives.

REVIEW

Circle the demonstrative adjectives in the sentences below.

- Draw an arrow from the demonstrative adjective to the noun it modifies.
- Circle the demonstrative adjective that would be used in Latin: **hic, haec, hoc** (A), **ille, illa, illud** (B), **iste, ista, istud** (C).

1. The Greeks planned to attack that city.   A   B   C

2. This plan was sure to work.   A   B   C

3. These ships are ready to sail.   A   B   C

4. Those ships are still under construction.   A   B   C

5. I do not like those (badly built) ships (of yours).   A   B   C

WHAT IS AN ADVERB?

An **ADVERB** is a word that describes a verb, an adjective, or another adverb. Adverbs indicate manner, quantity, intensity, time, or place.

> Theseus fights *well*.
> | |
>   verb adverb

> The labyrinth was *very* complicated.
> | |
>   adverb adjective

> Ariadne fell in love *too easily*.
> | |
>   adverb adverb

IN ENGLISH

There are different types of adverbs:

- **ADVERBS OF MANNER** answer the question *how*. These are the most common adverbs, and they are easy to recognize because they often end with -*ly*.
  Theseus escaped *cleverly*.
  Cleverly describes the verb *escaped*; it tells how Theseus escaped.

- **ADVERBS OF QUANTITY, INTENSITY** answer the question *how much*.
  Theseus feared *greatly*.

- **ADVERBS OF TIME** answer the question *when*.
  Theseus will come *soon*.

- **ADVERBS OF PLACE** answer the question *where*.
  The ship landed *there*.

Some words can function as an adverb or an adjective.

> Theseus ran *fast*.   Theseus escaped in a *fast* ship.
> | |
>   adverb   adjective
>   modifies verb *ran*   modifies noun *ship*

IN LATIN

Latin adverbs are **UNINFLECTED**; that is, they never change form. Some adverbs are formed from the adjective stem + the ending -**iter**, -**ē** or -**e** to indicate that the word is an adverb. Many adverbs, however, are different from their adjective counterparts, and you will have to learn them as vocabulary.

Just like adjectives, adverbs can have degrees of comparison: positive, comparative, and superlative. The meaning and formation of these degrees of comparison are very similar to the meaning and the formation of the comparative of adjectives (see *What is Meant by Comparison of Adjectives?*, p. 127); however, since adverbs do not change form, there is only one form for each degree. The most common adverbs have irregular comparisons similar to those of the adjectives which have irregular comparisons.

ADJECTIVE	bonus, -a, -um	melior, melius	optimus, -a, -um
	good	*better*	*best*
ADVERB	bene	melius	optimē
	well	*better*	*very well*

N.B. In English, some adverbs are identical in form with the corresponding adjective. It is important that you differentiate between the two parts of speech so that you will know which Latin form to use: the uninflected adverb or the adjective which agrees in case, gender, and number with the noun it modifies.

*Theseus ran **fast**.*	*Theseus escaped in a **fast** ship.*
Thēseus **celeriter** cucurrit.	Thēseus nāve **celerī** effūgit.
|	|
uninflected adverb	adjective fem. abl. sing.
modifies verb **cucurrit** *(ran)*	modifies noun **nāve** *(ship)*

 REVIEW

I. Circle the adverbs in the sentences below.
- Draw an arrow from the adverb to the word it modifies.
- Circle the part of speech the adverb modifies: verb (V), adjective (ADJ), adverb (ADV).

1. Theseus fought bravely.	V	ADJ	ADV
2. Ariadne loved him well, but not wisely.	V	ADJ	ADV
	V	ADJ	ADV
3. Theseus was too cruel to her.	V	ADJ	ADV
4. He abandoned her very carelessly.	V	ADJ	ADV
	V	ADJ	ADV

II. Circle whether the word in *italics* is an adjective (ADJ) or an adverb (ADV).

1. This is a *hard* surface.	ADJ	ADV
2. He worked very *hard*.	ADJ	ADV
3. You have *hardly* touched your food.	ADJ	ADV

WHAT IS AN INTERROGATIVE PRONOUN?

An INTERROGATIVE PRONOUN is a word that refers to a noun   1
and introduces a question. The word *interrogative*
comes from the Latin **inter** *(among)* + **rogāre** *(to ask)*.

> *Who* is coming for the banquet?
> |
> replaces a person or persons

> *What* did you eat at the banquet?
> |
> replaces a thing or things

IN ENGLISH
Different interrogative pronouns are used to ask about   10
persons and to ask about things.

PERSONS
The interrogative pronoun to ask about persons has three
different forms depending on its function in the sentence.

1. as subject → *who* (see *What is a Subject?*, p. 30)

> *Who* wrote that book?
> |
> subject

> *Who* will help you?
> |
> subject   20

Who is considered singular followed by a singular verb,
whether or not the expected answer is singular or plural.

> Who *is coming* tonight?
> |
> singular verb
> Mark *is coming* tonight. [singular answer]
> Mark and Julia *are coming* tonight. [plural answer]

2. as an object → *whom* (see *What are Objects?*, p. 36)

> *Whom* do you know here?   30
> |
> direct object

> *To whom* did you speak?
> |
> indirect object

> *From whom* did you get the book?
> |
> object of preposition *from*

3. as the possessive form → *whose*

> I found a stylus. *Whose* is it?
> |
>   possessive

> I have Mary's book. *Whose* do you have?
> |
>   possessive

Whose can refer to one or more persons. The answer can be in the singular or plural.

> *Whose* weapons are these?
> They are the soldier's. [singular answer]
> They are the soldiers'. [plural answer]

THINGS

There is only one interrogative pronoun to ask about

things → *what* [1]

> *What* is in the chest?
> |
> replaces a thing or things

What is considered singular followed by a singular verb, whether or not the expected answer is singular or plural.

> What *is* in the chest?
> |
> singular verb

> The treasure *is* in the chest. [singular answer]
> The treasures *are* in the chest. [plural answer]

DANGLING PREPOSITIONS (see *What is a Preposition?*, p. 18)

In English it is difficult to identify the function of pronouns that are indirect objects or objects of a preposition because the pronouns are often separated from the preposition. Consequently, in conversation the interrogative subject pronoun *who* is often used incorrectly instead of the interrogative object pronoun *whom*.

> *Who* did you give the book *to?*
> | |
> interrogative   dangling preposition
> pronoun

When a preposition is separated from its object and placed at the end of a sentence or question, it is called a **DANGLING PREPOSITION.**

To establish the function of an interrogative pronoun, you will have to change the structure of the sentence by moving the preposition from the end of the sentence or question and placing it before the interrogative pronoun.

---

[1]Do not confuse *what* as an interrogative pronoun with *what* as an interrogative adjective "*What* book is on the table?, see p. 135.

SPOKEN ENGLISH   →   RESTRUCTURED

Who did you speak *to?*   *To whom* did you speak?

instead of *whom*   preposition

Who did you get the book *from?*   *From whom* did you get the book?   80

instead of *whom*   preposition

IN LATIN

As in English, different interrogative pronouns are used to ask about persons and to ask about things.

PERSONS

The personal interrogative pronouns are fully declined in all cases. Unlike English where interrogative pronouns are singular with a singular verb regardless of the expected answer, Latin has a plural form for each case if a plural   90 answer is expected. Some cases have a different form for the masculine plural and the feminine plural if the questioner expects an answer referring to one of the genders, for example, a group of women (feminine plural).

To find the correct form of the interrogative pronoun, here is a series of steps to follow:

1. CASE: Determine the function of the interrogative pronoun to establish the case.
   - Is it the subject of the question?   *Who?* → nominative   100
   - Does it show possession?   *Whose?* → genitive
   - Is it the indirect object of the verb? *To/for whom?* → dative
   - Is it the direct object of the verb?   *Whom?* → accusative
   - Is it the object of a preposition?   *(With) whom?* → ablative
            (Against) whom? → accusative

2. NUMBER: Determine if the questioner is expecting a singular or plural answer.
   - SINGULAR — the questioner expects a singular answer → no gender distinction
   - PLURAL — the questioner expects a plural answer
     a) referring to a group of men or a mixed group of   110 men and women → masculine
     b) referring to a group of women only → feminine

3. SELECTION: Select an interrogative pronoun based on steps 1 and 2.

Here are a few examples. Since the English question does not reveal if the expected answer is singular, masculine plural or feminine plural, context is provided between brackets for each question below.

1. *who* → subject → nominative → **quis** (masc. and fem. sing.), **quī** (masc. pl.), **quae** (fem. pl.)

Who is in the dining room?
1. CASE: subject → nominative
2. NUMBER: singular

Quis est in trīclīniō? [expected answer: one person]
|
nom. sing.

Who is coming today?
1. CASE: subject → nominative
2. NUMBER & GENDER: plural masculine or feminine

Quī hodiē veniunt? [expected answer: many men/men + women]
|
nom. masc. pl.

Quae hodiē veniunt? [expected answer: many women]
|
nom. fem. pl.

2. *whom* → direct object → accusative → **quem** (masc. and fem. sing.), **quōs** (masc. pl.), **quās** (fem. pl.)

Whom do you see?
1. CASE: direct object → **vidēre** *(to see)* requires accusative
2. NUMBER: singular

Quem vidēs? [expected answer: one person]
|
acc. sing.

Whom is the soldier killing?
1. CASE: direct object → **necāre** *(to kill)* requires accusative
2. NUMBER & GENDER: masculine plural

Quōs mīles necat? [expected answer: many men]
|
acc. masc. pl.

3. *whom* → indirect object → dative → **cui** (sing.), **quibus** (pl.)

Whom shall I give the letter to?
RESTRUCTURED: *To whom shall I give the letter?*
1. CASE: indirect object → dative
2. NUMBER: singular

Cui epistulām dābō? [expected answer: one person]
|
dat. sing.

Whom are you giving the gifts to?
RESTRUCTURED: *To whom are you giving the gifts?*
1. CASE: indirect object → dative
2. NUMBER: plural

Quibus dōna dās? [expected answer: many people]
|
dat. pl.

Certain Latin verbs take a dative of indirect object, when the English verb takes an accusative object. The "to" idea is built into the meaning of the Latin verb.

Whom do you trust? [To whom do you give trust?]
    1. CASE: object in dative→ **crēdere** *(to trust)* requires dative
    2. NUMBER & GENDER: masculine or feminine singular
Cui crēdis? [expected answer: a man or a woman]
  |
dat. masc. or fem. sing.

4. *whom* → object of preposition → accusative or ablative
(depending on the preposition)   170
- preposition + accusative: **quem** (sing.), **quōs** (masc. pl.), **quās** (fem. pl.)
- preposition + ablative: **quō** (sing.), **quibus** (pl.)

Whom are you fighting against?
RESTRUCTURED: *Against whom are you fighting?*
    1. CASE: object of preposition **contrā** *(against)* → accusative
    2. NUMBER: singular
Contrā **quem** pugnās? [expected answer: singular]
  |
acc. sing.

Contrā **quōs** pugnās? [expected answer: many people]   180
  |
acc. masc. pl.

Contrā **quās** pugnās? [expected answer: many women]
  |
acc. fem. pl.

The interrogative pronoun as a direct object, an indirect object, or object of preposition is difficult to identify in English because *whom* is often replaced by *who*. To use the correct Latin form, restructure the English sentence in order to establish the correct function of the pronoun.

5. *whose* → possessive → genitive → **cuius** (sing.), **quōrum**   190
(masc. pl.), **quārum** (fem. pl.)

I have his book. Whose do you have?
    1. CASE: possessive → genitive
    2. NUMBER: singular
Librum eius habeō. **Cuius** habēs? [expected answer: one person]
  |
gen. sing.

N.B. The Latin equivalent of the interrogative *whose* is always an interrogative pronoun. Even if the question above were asked with *whose* as an adjective ("*Whose book* do you have?"), Latin would use the interrogative   200 pronoun, the word-for-word translation being "The book *of whom* do you have?"

I see jewels in the chest. **Whose** *are they?* [expected answer: the women's]
    1. CASE: possessive → genitive
    2. NUMBER: & GENDER: feminine plural
Gemmās in arcā videō. **Quārum** sunt?
            |
       gen. fem. pl.

THINGS

210   The interrogative pronouns referring to things are declined in all cases. However, there is only one gender, neuter: **quid** (sing.), **quae** (pl.).

To find the correct form of the interrogative pronoun, follow these two steps:

1. CASE: Determine the function of *what* in the question to establish the case.

2. NUMBER: If the questioner expects a singular answer choose the singular form, if a plural answer is expected, choose the plural form.

220   Here are a few examples.

What *is in the chest?* [expected answer: one thing]
    |
subject → nominative
Quid est in arcā?
   |
nom. sing.

What *do you see in the city?* [expected answer: many things]
    |
direct object → accusative
Quae in urbe vidēs?
  |
acc. pl.

 REVIEW

Fill in the blanks with the proper English form of *who* or *what*.
- Restructure sentences with dangling prepositions.
- Circle the appropriate Latin case for **quis** *(who)*, **quid** *(what)*: nominative (N), genitive (G), dative (D), accusative (A).

1. _____ is knocking at the door?   N G D A

2. _____ are you giving the roses to?   N G D A

   RESTRUCTURED: _____?

3. _____ is in the box?   N G D A

4. _____ did you see in the Forum?   N G D A

5. I found these books. _____ are they?   N G D A

6. _____ did you find in the box?   N G D A

WHAT IS A POSSESSIVE PRONOUN?

A POSSESSIVE PRONOUN is a word that replaces a noun [1]
and indicates the possessor of that noun. The word
possessive comes from *possess,* to own.

Whose house is that? It's *mine.*
  |
replaces the noun *house,* the thing possessed,
and shows who possesses it; *I own the house.*

IN ENGLISH
Here is a list of the possessive pronouns:

SINGULAR (ONE PERSON) POSSESSOR [10]

1ST PERSON		mine
2ND PERSON		yours
3RD PERSON	MASCULINE	his
	FEMININE	hers
	NEUTER	its

PLURAL (MORE THAN ONE PERSON) POSSESSOR

1ST PERSON	ours
2ND PERSON	yours
3RD PERSON	theirs

Possessive pronouns only refer to the possessor, not to the [20]
object possessed.

Is that your house? Yes, it is *mine.*
Are those your books? Yes, they are *mine.*
Although the things possessed are different, *house* is singular and *books* are plural, the same possessive pronoun *mine*
is used.

IN LATIN
The forms of the Latin possessive pronouns are the same
as those of the possessive adjective: **meus, -a, -um, etc.**
(my, etc.) declined in all cases (see pp. 132-3 in *What is a* [30]
Possessive Adjective?). As in English, a Latin possessive pronoun refers to the possessor. In addition, like all Latin
pronouns, it must agree in gender and number with the
person or thing possessed. The possessive pronoun's case will
depend on its function in the sentence.

To choose the correct form of possessive pronoun, follow
these steps.

1. POSSESSOR: Indicate the possessor with the stem of the possessive pronoun (same stem as possessive adjective).

SINGULAR

my	**me-**
your	**tu-**
his, her, its (own)	**su-**

PLURAL

our	**nostr-** (nom. sing. **noster**)
your	**vestr-** (nom. sing. **vester**)
their (own)	**su-**

2. NOUN POSSESSED: Identify the gender and number of the the noun possessed.

3. CASE: Determine the function of the possessive pronoun in the sentence.

4. SELECTION: Provide the ending which reflects the gender and number of the noun possessed and the function of the possessive pronoun.

Let us apply these steps to some examples.

*Is that your house? Yes, it is **mine**.*
1. POSSESSOR: 1ˢᵗ per. sing. → **me-**
2. NOUN POSSESSED GENDER & NUMBER: *house* → **domus** → feminine singular
3. CASE: predicate noun → nominative
4. SELECTION: **mea** → nominative feminine singular

Estne illa domus tua? Ita, est **mea**.

*Where are your children? I can see **ours**.*
1. POSSESSOR: 1ˢᵗ per. pl. → **nostr-**
2. NOUN POSSESSED GENDER & NUMBER: *children* → **līberī** → masculine plural
3. CASE: direct object → accusative
4. SELECTION: **nostrōs** → accusative masculine plural

Ubi sunt līberī vestrī? **Nostrōs** vidēre possum.

 REVIEW

Underline the possessive pronouns in the sentences below.
- Draw an arrow from the possessive pronoun to the noun possessed.
- Circle whether the noun possessed is singular (S) or plural (P).

1. Are those your daughters? Yes, they are mine.   S   P

2. Is this your house? Yes, it is mine.   S   P

3. Is this not our country? Yes, it is ours.   S   P

4. Is this our dog? No, it is yours.   S   P

5. Where are our sons? I see only yours.   S   P

WHAT IS A REFLEXIVE PRONOUN?

A REFLEXIVE PRONOUN is a pronoun which is the object of a verb and *reflects* back to the subject of the verb. [1]

Narcissus looks at *himself* in the pond.

subject = reflexive pronoun → the same person

IN ENGLISH

Reflexive pronouns end with *-self* in the singular and *-selves* in the plural.

	SUBJECT PRONOUN	REFLEXIVE PRONOUN	
SINGULAR			[10]
1ST PERSON	I	myself	
2ND PERSON	you	yourself	
3RD PERSON	he	himself	
	she	herself	
	it	itself	
PLURAL			
1ST PERSON	we	ourselves	
2ND PERSON	you	yourselves	
3RD PERSON	they	themselves	[20]

Reflexive pronouns can have a variety of functions: direct and indirect objects, objects of a preposition.

- direct object

  I cut *myself* with my sword.

  I is the subject of *cut; myself* (same person) → direct object

- indirect object

  You should give *yourself* a present.

  You is the subject of *should give; yourself* (same person) → indirect object [30]

- object of preposition

  They talk too much about *themselves*.

  They is the subject of *talk; themselves* (same persons) → object of the preposition *about*

IN LATIN

As in English, there are reflexive pronouns for each of the different personal pronouns. Each reflexive pronoun is fully declined in all cases. As in English, the reflexive pronouns can have a variety of functions: direct and indirect objects, objects of a preposition.

Mē gladiō meō secuī.
|
reflexive pronoun
direct object → accusative
*I cut **myself** with my sword.*

Tibi dōnum dare dēbēs.
|
reflexive pronoun
indirect object → dative
*You ought to give **yourself** a present.*

Contrā sē pugnāvit.
|
reflexive pronoun
object of preposition **contrā** *(against)* → accusative
*He fought against **himself**.*

SUMMARY

Below is a chart of reflexive pronouns you can use as reference.

SUBJECT PRONOUNS		REFLEXIVE PRONOUNS				
Nominative		Genitive	Dative	Accusative	Ablative	
				SINGULAR		
1	ego	meī	mihi	mē	mē	*myself*
2	tū	tuī	tibi	tē	tē	*yourself*
3	is ea id	suī	sibi	sē	sē	*himself herself itself*
				PLURAL		
1	nōs	nostrī	nōbīs	nōs	nōbīs	*ourselves*
2	vōs	vestrī	vōbīs	vōs	vōbīs	*yourselves*
3	eī eae ea	suī	sibi	sē	sē	*themselves*

✎ REVIEW

Circle the reflexive pronouns in the sentences below.

■ Circle whether each reflexive pronoun is the 1st, 2nd, or 3rd person singular (S) or plural (P).

1. No one hates himself.	1	2	3	S	P
2. All people love themselves.	1	2	3	S	P
3. I see myself in the window.	1	2	3	S	P
4. You see yourself in the window.	1	2	3	S	P
5. We see ourselves in our parents.	1	2	3	S	P
6. You see yourselves in your children.	1	2	3	S	P

CHAPTER

47

WHAT IS A DEMONSTRATIVE PRONOUN?

A DEMONSTRATIVE PRONOUN is a word that replaces a noun as if pointing to it. The word *demonstrative* comes from the Latin **dēmōnstrāre** meaning *to point out* or *show*.

Choose a path. *This (one)* is hard. *That (one)* is easy.
  | └───┬───┘   └───┬───┘
antecedent   points to a path   points to another path

In English and Latin, demonstrative pronouns can function in a variety of ways, as subjects or as objects.

IN ENGLISH

The singular demonstrative pronouns are *this (one)* and *that (one)*; the plural forms are *these* and *those*.

The distinction between *this* and *that* can be used to contrast one object with another, or to refer to things that are not the same distance away. The speaker uses *this* or *these* for the closer objects and *that* or *those* for the ones farther away.

Cupid has two arrows. *This one* is sharp; *that one* is dull.
  | └──┬──┘   └──┬──┘
antecedent   close at hand   at a distance

"*These* are my weapons," says Cupid, "I do not employ *those*."
  | |
referring to the arrows   referring to the stones
at hand   at a distance

IN LATIN

The forms of the Latin demonstrative pronouns are the same as those of demonstrative adjectives: **hic, haec, hoc** (*this*) and **ille, illa, illud** (*that*) declined in all cases (see *What is a Demonstrative Adjective?*, p. 138). Since they are pronouns, instead of modifying nouns as adjectives do, they replace them.

The form of the demonstrative pronoun depends on a series of factors: the function of the pronoun in the sentence, the gender of the pronoun's antecedent, and the idea being expressed.

To choose the correct form, follow these steps.

1. CASE: Determine the function of the demonstrative pronoun in the sentence to establish the case.

2. GENDER: Determine the antecedent and its gender.
3. NUMBER: Determine the number of the idea being expressed:
   - if the idea is *this (one)* or *that (one)* → singular
   - if the idea is *these* or *those* → plural
4. SELECTION: Select the proper form of the demonstrative pronoun based on steps 1-3.

Let us apply these steps to some examples.

> *Cupid has two arrows.* **This (one)** *is sharp;* **that (one)** *is dull.*
> 1. CASE: *This (one)* and *that (one)* → both subjects → nominative
> 2. GENDER: antecedent → **sagittās** *(arrows)* → feminine
> 3. NUMBER: *This (one)* and *that (one)* → both singular
> 4. SELECTION: nominative feminine singular → **haec** and **illa**
> Cupīdo duās sagittās habet. **Haec** est acūta; **illa** est obtūsa.
>   fem.   nom. fem. sing.   nom. fem. sing.

> *"*These *are my weapons," says Cupid. "I do not employ* **those.***"*
> 1. CASE: *These* → subject → nominative; *those* → direct object → accusative
> 2. GENDER: antecedent → **arma** *(weapons)* → neuter
> 3. NUMBER: *These* and *those* → both plural
> 4. SELECTION: accusative neuter plural → **haec** and **illa**
> *"***Haec** *sunt mea arma," dīcit Cupīdo. "***Illa** *nōn adhibeō."*
>   nom. neut. pl.   neut.   acc. neut. pl.

✎ REVIEW

Circle the demonstrative pronouns in the sentences below.
- Draw an arrow from the demonstrative pronoun to the noun to which it refers.
- Circle the gender and number you would use for each equivalent Latin pronoun: masculine (M), feminine (F), or neuter (N), and singular (S) or plural (P). (Where necessary, the Latin antecedent and its gender have been indicated.)

1. This is a stupid plan. (**consilium**, *n.*)   M F N S P

2. Those are not my daughters.   M F N S P

3. This is not a sharp arrow. (**sagitta**, *f.*)   M F N S P

4. That is not my boyfriend.   M F N S P

5. These are our faithful wives.   M F N S P

6. My soldiers are faithful,
   but I do not trust those (men).   M F N S P

7. My wife is faithful,
   but I do not trust that one.   M F N S P

156

CHAPTER

48

WHAT IS A RELATIVE PRONOUN?

A **RELATIVE PRONOUN** is a word used at the beginning of a clause giving additional information about someone or something previously mentioned.

clause
additional information about *the book*

I'm reading the book *that* the teacher recommended.

A relative pronoun serves two purposes:

1. As a pronoun it stands for a noun previously mentioned. The noun to which it refers is called the **ANTECEDENT.**

subordinate clause

This is the woman *who* caused the war.

antecedent of the relative pronoun *who*

2. It introduces a **SUBORDINATE CLAUSE**; that is, a group of words having a subject and a verb which cannot stand alone because it does not express a complete thought. A subordinate clause is dependent on a **MAIN CLAUSE**; that is, another group of words having a subject and a verb which can stand alone as a complete sentence (see p. 103).

main clause   subordinate clause

Helen is the woman *who caused the war.*

subject verb   subject verb

A subordinate clause that starts with a relative pronoun is also called a **RELATIVE CLAUSE**. In the example above, the relative clause starts with the relative pronoun *who* and gives us additional information about the antecedent *Helen.*

IN ENGLISH

Different relative pronouns are used according to whether they refer to a person or to a thing.

PERSONS

The relative pronoun *who* is used when the antecedent is a person. It has different forms depending on its function in the relative clause.

1. as subject → *who* (see *What is a Subject?*, p. 30)

> This is the hero *who* won the war.
> | |
> antecedent subject of *won*

2. as an object → *whom* (see *What are Objects?*, p. 36). We have indicated *whom* between parentheses because it is often omitted in English.

> This is the hero *(whom)* Hector killed.
> | |
> antecedent object of *killed*

3. as the possessive form → *whose*

> Helen was the woman *whose* beauty started the war.
> | |
> antecedent possessive modifying *beauty*

THINGS

The relative pronouns *which* or *that* are used when the antecedent is a thing. We have indicated them between parentheses because they are often omitted in English.

> Troy is the city *(which)* the Greeks destroyed.
> Troy is the city *(that)* the Greeks destroyed.
> |
> antecedent

COMBINING SENTENCES WITH RELATIVE PRONOUNS

A relative pronoun allows us to combine two thoughts which have a common element into a single sentence. Notice that the antecedent always stands immediately before the relative pronoun which introduces the relative clause.

1. relative pronoun as subject

> **SENTENCE A** That is the *hero*.
> **SENTENCE B** *He* won the war.

You can combine Sentences A and B by replacing the subject pronoun *he* with the relative pronoun *who*.

> relative clause
> ┌──────┴──────┐
> That is the hero *who* won the war.
> | |
> antecedent relative pronoun subject of relative clause

2. relative pronoun as object

> **SENTENCE A** This is the *hero*.
> **SENTENCE B** *Hector* killed him.

You can combine Sentences A and B by replacing the object pronoun *him* with the relative pronoun *whom*.

> relative clause
> ┌──────┴──────┐
> This is the hero *(whom)* Hector killed.
> | |
> antecedent relative pronoun
> person object of the verb *killed*

40

50

60

70

80

relative clause

This is the battle *(that)* Achilles won.

antecedent   relative pronoun
thing   object of the verb *won*

We have placed *whom* and *that* between parentheses because relative pronoun objects are often omitted in English. You will have to reinstate them because they must be expressed in Latin.

3. relative pronoun as object of a preposition

SENTENCE A   Helen is a beautiful *woman.*
SENTENCE B   Paris ran away with *her.*

You can combine Sentences A and B by replacing the preposition *(with)* + *her* with the preposition *(with)* + relative pronoun *whom.*

relative clause

Helen is the beautiful woman *with whom* Paris ran away.

antecedent   relative pronoun
person   object of preposition *with*

In colloquial English, Sentences A and B could have been combined without a relative pronoun and with a dangling preposition (see pp. 144-5).

Helen is the beautiful woman Paris ran away *with.*

Since a relative pronoun must always be expressed in Latin, it is important that you reinstate it. This can easily be done if you remember that the preposition and relative pronoun always follow the antecedent. In the above sentence, placing the preposition *with* after the antecedent *woman (woman with)* will help you to reinstate the relative pronoun *(whom)* in the proper case in English and avoid the dangling preposition.

IN LATIN

The relative pronoun **quī**, **quae**, **quod**, declined in all cases, is used to refer to persons or things.

The form of the relative pronoun depends on a series of factors: not only on whether the antecedent is a person or thing, but also the grammatical gender of the antecedent, and its number. Its case is determined by its use in its own relative clause. To choose the correct form, follow these steps.

1. RELATIVE CLAUSE: Identify the relative clause.

   ▪ Reinstate the relative pronoun if it has been omitted from the English sentence.

- Restructure the English sentence if there is a dangling preposition.
2. CASE: Determine the function of the relative pronoun in the relative clause to establish the case.
3. GENDER & NUMBER: Identify the antecedent and its gender and number.
4. SELECTION: Select the proper form of the relative pronoun based on steps 1-3.

Let us apply these steps to some examples.

*The woman **who** caused the war was Helen.*
 1. RELATIVE CLAUSE: *who* caused the war
 2. CASE: *who* → subject → nominative
 3. GENDER & NUMBER: antecedent → **fēmina** *(woman)* → feminine singular
 4. SELECTION: nominative feminine singular → **quae**
Fēmina **quae** causam bellī dedit erat Helena.

      nom. fem. sing.

*Is this the kingdom **(that)** the Greeks destroyed?*
 1. RELATIVE CLAUSE: *that* the Greeks destroyed
 2. CASE: *that* → direct object → accusative
 3. GENDER & NUMBER: antecedent → **rēgnum** *(kingdom)* → neuter singular
 4. SELECTION: accusative neuter singular → **quod**
Hocne est rēgnum **quod** Graecī vastāvērunt?

      acc. neut. sing.

*Circe, **whose** power was very great, kept Ulysses in her palace.*
 1. RELATIVE CLAUSE: *whose* power was very great
 2. CASE: *whose* → possessive modifier connecting Circe with her power → genitive
 3. GENDER & NUMBER: antecedent → **Circē** *(Circe)* → feminine singular
 4. SELECTION: genitive feminine singular → **cuius**
Circē, **cuius** potentia erat maxima, Ulixem in rēgiā retinēbat.

      gen. fem. sing.

*Where is the woman you ran away **with**?*
RESTRUCTURED: *Where is the woman **with whom** you ran away?*
 1. RELATIVE CLAUSE: *with whom* you ran away
 2. CASE: *whom* → object of preposition *with* → **cum** always takes an ablative object
 3. GENDER & NUMBER: antecedent → **fēmina** *(woman)* → feminine singular
 4. SELECTION: ablative feminine singular → **quā**
Ubi est fēmina **quācum** confūgistī?

      abl. fem. sing. → **cum** *(with)* is attached to **quā**

The temples (which) we are visiting are very beautiful.
1. RELATIVE CLAUSE: *which* we are visiting
2. CASE: *which* → direct object → accusative
3. GENDER & NUMBER: antecedent → **templa** *(temples)* → neuter plural
4. SELECTION: accusative neuter plural → **quae**

Templa **quae** vīsitāmus sunt pulcherrima.
⎜
acc. neut. pl.

These are the swords you were talking about.
RESTRUCTURED: *These are the swords about which you were talking.*
1. RELATIVE CLAUSE: *about which* you were talking
2. CASE: *which* → object of preposition *about* → **dē** always takes an ablative object.
3. GENDER & NUMBER: antecedent → **gladiī** *(swords)* → masculine plural
4. SELECTION: ablative masculine plural → **quibus**

Hī sunt gladiī **dē quibus** loquēbāris.
⎜
abl. masc. pl.

N.B. Relative pronouns must always be expressed in Latin, although they are sometimes omitted in English. In Latin, the relative pronoun takes its gender and number from its antecedent, but takes its case from its function in its own relative clause.

 REVIEW

I. Restructure the sentences below to avoid dangling prepositions and to supply the missing relative pronoun.
- Underline the relative pronoun.
- Circle the antecedent.

1. This is the hero we were talking about.

_____

2. Aeneas is the leader they came with.

_____

3. Dido is the queen he gave gifts to.

_____

II. Fill in *who* or *whom* in the sentences below.
1. Aeneas married Dido _____ loved him.
2. Aeneas married Dido _____ he later abandoned.
3. Aeneas heeded the words of Mercury _____ he respected.
4. Mercury reminded Aeneas about the gods _____ he had neglected.

WHAT IS AN INTERJECTION?

An INTERJECTION is a cry, an expression of strong feeling
or emotion which usually appears, i.e. "is thrown into,"
at or near the beginning of the sentence. The term comes
from the Latin **interjectum** *(thrown into)*.

IN ENGLISH

There is a great variety of emotional words, including
most words of swearing and profanity. They belong to
both written and spoken language. When written, they
are separated from the main clause by a comma; the sentence usually ends with an exclamation mark.

> *Ah,* how beautiful she is!
> *Alas,* wretched me!

IN LATIN

A similar variety of emotional words exists in Latin and
includes the equivalents of expressions of awe, anger, and
the evoking of a deity. An interjection is invariable; i.e., it
never changes form.

> **A,** quam pulchra est!
> *Ah, how beautiful she is!*
>
> **Heu,** mē miserum!
> *Alas, wretched me!*
>
> Periī, **hercule**; nōmen perdidī!
> *I've died, **by Hercules;** I've lost my name!*

2. What is a Noun? 1. Diana, goddess, moon; 2. Phoebus Apollo, brother, god, sun; 3. Mars, god, war; 4. Juno, goddess, marriage, childbirth; 5. deities, Mt. Olympus, Olympians

3. What is Meant by Gender? 1. F; 2. M; 3. N; 4. M; 5. F; 6. F; 7. M; 8. N; 9. F; 10. M

4. What is Meant by Number? 1. alumnae; 2. alumnī; 3. annī; 4. templa; 5. litterae; 6. curricula; 7. portae; 8. animī; 9. rosae; 10. cōdicēs

7. What is a Preposition? 1. to Perseus → IO; 2. to Gorgon country → PP; 3. of Medusa → G; 4. with the Gorgon head → PP; 5. to the king → IO; 6. from the power → PP; of the evil king → G

8. What is Meant by Case? 1. N, Acc, Acc; 2. ABL, N, Acc; 3. N, G, N, Acc, D, G

9. What is a Subject? 1. Q: Who is the goddess of the sacred fire? A: Vesta → S; 2. Q: Who tend the sacred fire? A: Vestal Virgins → P; 3. Q: What stands in the Forum? A: temple → S

10. What is a Predicate Word? (Linking verb, predicate word, subject) 1. are, angry, goddesses; 2. is, god, Apollo; 3. is, daughter, Daphne; 4. is, he, it; 5. are, enemies, these

11. What is the Possessive? 1. Arachne's → PG; 2. of Minerva → PG; 3. of weaving → OG; 4. Minerva's → PG; 5. of the forest → PG

12. What are Objects? 1. Q: The king abandoned whom? A: His daughter → DO Q: The king abandoned his daughter in what (where)? A: In the woods → OP; 2. Q: Wild animals raised whom? A: Atalanta → DO; 3. Q: Atalanta went to what? A: The palace → OP; 4. The king gave what? A: His blessing → DO; Q: The king gave his blessing to whom? A: To Atalanta → IO

13. What is a Personal Pronoun? I. 1. you → vōs; 2. they → eī; 3. we → nōs; 4. them → eās; 5. her → eam II. 1. it → F, S, Acc; 2. they → M, P, Nom; 3. it → N, S, Acc

14. What is a Verb ? 1. praises → v.t.; 2. is watching → v.t.; 3. was running → v.i.; 4. loved → v.t.; 5. kills → v.t.

15. What are the Principal Parts of a Verb? I. 1. thought, thought; 2. ran, run; 3. drove, driven II. **laudō**, I praise, am praising, do praise; **laudāre**, to praise; **laudāvī**, I praised, have praised, did praise; **laudātus, -a, -um**, having been praised

16. What is an Infinitive? 1. gave → to give;　2. knew → to know;　3. was → to be; saw → to see　4. dug → to dig; whispered → to whisper; sang → to sing

17. What is a Verb Conjugation? I. 1.k āre → 1ˢᵗ;　2. ere → 3ʳᵈ; 3. ēre → 2ⁿᵈ;　4. īre → 4ᵗʰ;　5. ere → 3ʳᵈ　II. STEM: laudā- PRESENT TENSE: laudō, *I praise*; laudās, *you (sing.) praise*; laudat, *he, she, it praises*; laudāmus, *we praise*; laudātis, *you (pl.) praise*; laudant, *they praise*

18. What is Meant by Tense? I. PRESENT: I think;　PAST: I thought; FUTURE: I shall (will) think;　PRESENT PERFECT: I have thought; PAST PERFECT: I had thought;　FUTURE PERFECT: I shall (will) have thought;　II. They eat; they ate; they will eat; they have eaten; they had eaten; they will have eaten

19. What is the Present Tense? 1. PROGRESSIVE: The girls are carrying the sacred water. EMPHATIC: The girls do carry the sacred water. QUESTION: Are the girls carrying the sacred water? or Do the girls carry the sacred water?; 2. PROGRESSIVE: The Vestal Virgin is taking care of the sacred fire. EMPHATIC: The Vestal Virgin does take care of the sacred fire; QUESTION: Is the Vestal Virgin taking care of the sacred fire? or Does the Vestal Virgin take care of the sacred fire?; 3. PROGRESSIVE: The Vestal Virgins are living in a sacred building; EMPHATIC: The Vestal Virgins do live in a sacred building; QUESTION: Are the Vestal Virgins living in a sacred building? or Do the Vestal Virgins live in a sacred building?

20. What is the Past Tense? IMPERFECT: was sitting, was sleeping, was, was, was working, was sleeping;　PERFECT: heard, sat up, barked, ran, called, arrived, foundh

21. What is the Past Perfect Tense? 1. (-1) I, (-2) PP;　2. (-2) PP (-1) I;　3. (-1) I, (-2) PP;　4. (-1) P; (-2), PP

22. What is the Future Tense? 1. ENGLISH: P, F;　LATIN: F, F; 2. ENGLISH: P, F;　LATIN: F, F;　3. ENGLISH: F, P;　LATIN: F, F

23. What is the Future Perfect Tense? 1. ENGLISH: F, P;　LATIN: F, F; 2. ENGLISH: FP, P;　LATIN: FP, F;　3. ENGLISH: P, FP;　LATIN: F, FP

24. What is an Auxiliary Verb? demanded (V); was (V); asked (V); (to drive is an infinitive); was feeling (VP); had requested (VP); insisted (V); yoked (V); could feel (VP); plunged (V); was burned (VP); was frozen (VP); hurled (V), was killed (VP)

25. What is a Participle? 1. growing, A;　2. left, VP;　3. desiring, A;　4. chosen, VP;　5. chosen, A

26. What is a Gerund? 1. hoping, P; 2. training, G; 3. training, VP; 4. escaping, G; 5. dancing, G

27. What is Meant by Active and Passive Voice? 1. were falling, A; 2. were raked, P; 3. did carry, A; 4. were given, P; 5. Has . . . been given, P; 6. Will . . . be announced, P

29. What is the Imperative Mood? 1. sow (S); 2. go on board (P); 3. Let . . . obey (S); 4. Let . . . not forget (P); 5. do not kill (S)

31. What is a Conjunction? 1. after (SC); 2. Because (SC); 3. After (P); 4. Before (P); 5. Because of (P); 6. Before (SC)

32. What are Sentences, Phrases, and Clauses? I. 1. C; 2. C; 3. Cx II. 1. P; 2. C; 3. S; 4. S

33. What What are Declarative, Interrogative, Affirmative, and Negative Sentences? I. 1. Did the Greeks win the war? The Greeks did not win the war.   2. Did Helen love Paris? Helen did not love Paris. 3. Will Helen return home? Helen will not return home.   II. Helen loved Paris, didn't she?; Helen did not love Paris, did she?

34. What is Meant by Direct and Indirect Statements? 1. Cassandra says that Troy is falling.   2. Cassandra thought that the Trojan women had been slaves. 3. Cassandra told the king that his wife would kill them. II. 1. "I am in danger." 2. "He no longer loves me." 3. "His friends [have] killed him."   III. 1. that his friends love him. = PI; that his friends loved him. = PI; 2. that his friends loved him. – PFI; that his friends had loved him. – PFI; 3. that his friends will love him. + FI; that his friends would love him. + FI

35. What is Meant by Direct and Indirect Questions? I. 1. Clytemnestra asked why her daughter was being taken. 2. Agamemnon asked why his daugher was being sacrificed. 3. Iphigenia wondered why the priests were standing there. II. 1. SEC; 2. SEC; 3. PRIM; 4. PRIM; 5. PRIM

36. What are Conditional Sentences? 1. S; 2. SW; 3. CF; 4. CF; 5. SW

38. What is a Descriptive Adjective? 1. heroic → F, S, NOM; strong → M, S, NOM; 2. mad → M, S, NOM; faithful → F, S, ACC; 3. evil → N, S, ACC; harsh → M, P, ACC II. 1. A; 2. B 2; 3. A; 4. B 2; 5. B 1; 6. B 3; 7. B 2

39. What is Meant by Comparison of Adjectives? 1. thicker → blood, C; 2. best → friends, S; 3. famous → poet, P; 4. more famous → poets, C; 5. most famous → poet, S

40. What is a Possessive Adjective? 1. our, mothers, direct object → accusative, F, P, **nostrās** 2. your, mothers, direct object → accusative, F, P, **vestrās** 3. their (own), R, mothers, direct object → accusative, F, P, **suās** 4. their (boyfriends), Non-R, genitive, boyfriends, M, P, **eōrum**

41. What is the Interrogative Adjective? 1. what → man, A; 2. what kind of → man, B; 3. what kind of → crime, B; 4. how much → booty, C; 5. how many → years, D; 6. how many → Trojans, D

42. What is a Demonstrative Adjective? 1. that → city, B; 2. this → plan, A; 3. these → ships, A; 4. those → ships, B; 5. those → ships, C

43. What is an Adverb? I. 1. bravely → fought, V; 2. well → loved, V; wisely → loved, V; 3. too → cruel, ADJ; 4. very → carelessly, ADV; carelessly → abandoned, V II. 1. hard → ADJ 2. hard → ADV 3. hardly → ADV

44. What is an Interrogative Pronoun? 1. Who → N; 2. Whom → D RESTRUCTURED: To whom are you giving roses?; 3. What → N; 4. Whom or What → A; 5. Whose → G; 6. What → A

45. What is a Possessive Pronoun? 1. mine → daughters, P; 2. mine → house, S; 3. ours → country, S; 4 . yours → dog, S; 5. yours → sons, P

46. What is a Reflexive Pronoun? 1. himself, 3, S; 2. themselves, 3, P; 3. myself, 1, S; 4. yourself, 2, S; 5. ourselves, 1, P; 6. yourselves, 2, P

47. What is a Demonstrative Pronoun? 1. this → plan, N, S; 2. those → daughters, F, P; 3. this → arrow, F, S; 4. that → boyfriend, M, S; 5. these → wives, F, P; 6. those → soldiers, M, P; 7. that (one) → F, S

48. What is a Relative Pronoun? I. 1. This is the hero about whom we were talking. (whom) → hero; 2. Aeneas is the leader with whom they came. (whom) → leader; 3. Dido is the queen to whom he gave the gifts. (whom) → queen II. 1. who 2. whom 3. whom 4. whom